SO YOU WANT to be an author? With detailed but digestible discussions, Kathleen A. Kendall-Tackett provides a remarkable list of tricks of the trade—on topics such as planning, designing, writing, and editing a book or an article; dealing with editors; obtaining a contract (a *good* contract); marketing; and performing all of the other steps from start to finish.

— **Gary B. Melton, PhD,** *Professor and Director, Institute on Family & Neighborhood Life, Clemson University, Clemson, SC*

THIS CLEARLY WRITTEN BOOK, which was also a pleasure to read, could be renamed *Everything You Always Wanted to Know About Writing and Publishing for a General Audience.* It provides essential knowledge and could serve as a "cook book" for writers. I write in the scholarly literature, and I have never written a trade book for a lay audience. Kendall-Tackett made me feel I could. In fact, I think I will.

— **Judith L. Alpert, PhD,** *President, Division of Trauma Psychology, American Psychological Association; Professor of Applied Psychology, New York University, New York, NY*

THINKING ABOUT making your work more accessible for a general audience? Then *How to Write for a General Audience* is for you. Using a conversational tone, spiced with witty prose and the benefit of her own vast personal experiences, Kathleen A. Kendall-Tackett takes the reader through key style differences between academic and general audience writing. She also gives practical, nuts-and-bolts information needed to effectively shop your ideas around, work with editors, develop good book proposals, and negotiate (and stick to) contractual agreements. Every scholar who wants to cross over to general audience writing needs this book!

— **L. Kevin Hamberger, PhD,** *Professor, Department of Family and Community Medicine, Medical College of Wisconsin, Milwaukee*

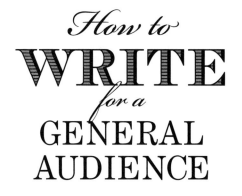

How to
WRITE
for a
GENERAL
AUDIENCE

How to WRITE *for a* GENERAL AUDIENCE

A Guide for Academics Who Want to Share Their Knowledge With the World and Have Fun Doing It

KATHLEEN A. KENDALL-TACKETT, PHD

APA
Life Tools
American Psychological Association
Washington, DC

Published by
American Psychological Association
750 First Street, NE
Washington, DC 20002
www.apa.org

To order   Tel: (800) 374-2721; Direct: (202) 336-5510
APA Order Department   Fax: (202) 336-5502; TDD/TTY: (202) 336-6123
P.O. Box 92984   Online: www.apa.org/books/
Washington, DC 20090-2984   E-mail: order@apa.org

In the U.K., Europe, Africa, and the Middle East, copies may be ordered from
American Psychological Association
3 Henrietta Street
Covent Garden, London
WC2E 8LU England

Typeset in Minion and Goudy by World Composition Services, Inc., Sterling, VA

Printer: Sheridan Books, Ann Arbor, MI
Cover Designer: Naylor Design, Washington, DC
Technical/Production Editor: Harriet Kaplan

The opinions and statements published are the responsibility of the authors, and such opinions and statements do not necessarily represent the policies of the American Psychological Association.

Library of Congress Cataloging-in-Publication Data

Kendall-Tackett, Kathleen A.
    How to write for a general audience : a guide for academics who want to share their knowledge with the world and have fun doing it / by Kathleen A. Kendall-Tackett.
        p. cm.
    Includes bibliographical references and index.
    ISBN-13: 978-0-9792125-3-6
    ISBN-10: 0-9792125-3-7
    1. Authorship. 2. Authorship—Marketing. 3 Academic writing. I. Title.
    PN145.K38 2007
    808′.02—dc22   2007010275

British Library Cataloguing-in-Publication Data
A CIP record is available from the British Library.

Printed in the United States of America
First Edition

Contents

Foreword

I wish Kathleen Kendall-Tackett had titled this book, *A Guide for Anyone Who Wants to Publish Their Work*! I say this because her suggestions and techniques are appropriate for all authors—not only scholars who want to write for a general audience but also those who want to publish in professional journals.

When I was in junior and senior high school, I wrote all of the time and enjoyed it. I liked to write stories, articles, and even papers (OK, I was a little weird then!). College, though, changed all of this. My required English courses eliminated all of my desire to write and took the fun away, because no matter what I wrote or how I did it, it was judged to be wrong. I stopped writing for several years except for required papers. Then I entered graduate school, and my enjoyment of writing returned because I wanted to express my ideas, publish research and other articles, and challenge myself. This worked well until dissertation time. Writing and finishing my dissertation, all 280 pages of it, in a relatively short period of time in order to graduate and begin my professorial life, burned me out for writing. This is not unusual, unfortunately, in that most professionals never publish any articles, and those who do only publish their dissertation. The dissertation process does that to people! In fact, I did not write anything else for more than 3 years.

I finally had to force myself to begin to write again because I wanted to publish some of my research studies. It was a painful process. I wish I had had the information in the present book at the time, because it would likely have made things easier for me. I gradually became more comfortable with writing and published both formal articles in professional journals and informal ones in bulletins and newsletters. I realized that I could write, but writing never produced the enjoyment for me that it had when I was an adolescent. Even now, it is sometimes more work than fun, but a necessary part of my life. I should point out that I have now written or edited several books and journal articles, and I edit four scholarly journals and a bulletin. I also train professionals in how to publish in professional journals and books. Thus, I think the points raised in the present book should be taken seriously and will be helpful whether you want to write for professional journals or for a general audience.

There are many commonalities in writing, no matter who the audience might be. First, the writing must convey a meaningful message and contribute to the knowledge base. It should also be readable. Somehow, and I am not sure when or why, it was determined that professional writing in journals had to be dull, boring, and technical and had to contain jargon. The more boring and technical the style, then the more professional the article must be! This never made much sense to me, but I fell into the same trap as most academics and followed the "rules." It has only been in the past decade, after editing several journals and books, that I realized many of these rules were really not necessary. I realized, as Kendall-Tackett has pointed out in the present book, that making one's writing more vibrant and interesting than has been the academic norm is appropriate for many journals now, and good editors understand this. Putting on my editor hat, I think there are just three useful distinctions between writing for professional versus general audiences. A chatty first-person tone, such as the one I have used in this foreword, is not appropriate for professional publications. In addition, professional writing is not usually in the narrative, nor does it emphasize stories. Finally, professional writing uses many more references and citations to support the statements being made.

Many elements of a piece of writing that are not usually thought appropriate for professional writing, however, can add a great deal of value. It is indeed important to know what message you are trying to disseminate, the implications and meaning from the research, and the usefulness of the findings. Quotes, boxes, figures, and tables are helpful for all writing to make the manuscript visually friendly, readable, and clearer. Whatever you write, it should be something you would enjoy reading.

Whatever your style, it is important when writing for both general and professional audiences to take the reader on a journey that is interesting, that flows, and that makes sense. Read and review the journals, books, or magazines in which you want to publish. Learn what the editors want and the style their writers use, and follow their lead. For example, determine whether they emphasize or discourage stories or case examples.

It is also valuable for every writer to know his or her strengths. This book addresses the important topic of collaboration (see chap. 5). Sometimes collaboration is a good way to obtain the best outcome. I enjoy collaborating and do this on most writing projects. I am a better editor than writer, even though I write a lot by most standards. I learned a while ago that my strength is editing, so I usually link with someone who is a strong writer, and the combination produces a better manuscript. Linking with someone who has published before is also a good way to get more experience publishing when you first get started.

Kendall-Tackett brings up many specific issues to consider when writing and publishing. One is determining whether you want to write for the general audience (i.e., trade books), the professional audience (scholarly publishers), or for a broad-based audience that includes both (crossover books). Once this decision is made, then you can move to the next step of writing. Many good suggestions are given in the present book to deal with things that get in the way of writing; the key is that all writers experience such setbacks. Kendall-Tackett's overall advice is geared toward keeping the process moving forward.

In addition to providing advice about writing, Kendall-Tackett addresses the realities of getting your work published and noticed. She offers sound advice on a range of issues, such as dealing with rejections, negotiating contracts, and doing your part to publicize your work. Once you submit a manuscript, be prepared for rejections. Almost all of us have received rejections, and it is not unusual to get more of these in the early stages of publishing. Consider yourself fortunate if you receive a revise-and-resubmit comment from an editor in the early stage of submitting manuscripts. This means that the editor believes your manuscript has merit and has a chance of being published, especially if you follow the suggestions by the reviewers and editors. This is actually a very positive response. As long as the editor is suggesting you resubmit, even if it is the third revision, continue to do so. It is likely the manuscript will be published.

Trainings and presentations related to your book topic, once it is published, can sometimes bring in more funds than the book royalties themselves. It is important not to be shy with marketing, because you want people to buy and read your book. Kendall-Tackett offers many strong suggestions for book promotion.

In summary, this book provides an enjoyable journey for the reader who wants to write and publish. Many good techniques, advice for overcoming obstacles, and practical tips are presented here. Kendall-Tackett has provided a worthwhile resource for all those attempting to publish their work. I wish I had had such a resource when I began writing.

Robert Geffner, PhD, ABPN, ABPP
President, Institute on Violence, Abuse and Trauma, and Clinical Research Professor, Alliant International University, San Diego, CA; Editor-in-Chief, Trauma and Maltreatment Program, Haworth Press

Acknowledgments

Books are never created in a vacuum. There are always people working behind the scenes to bring them to life. The same is true for this volume. I'd like to start by thanking my wonderful writing instructors at Stanford University. To Bruce Henderson, David Elias, and Arthur Hall: Thanks for the many hours you spent helping me find my voice.

I'd also like to thank Susan Reynolds, senior acquisitions editor at the American Psychological Association, for believing in this project and guiding me through the process. As usual, she has been a pleasure to work with. Many thanks also to Linda McCarter, development and acquisitions editor at the American Psychological Association, for gently guiding me through the editing phase.

I've been fortunate to be surrounded by colleagues who generously share their wisdom and experiences with others. You'll read some of their stories in this book. Many thanks to Tom Hale, Teresa Pitman,

Rachel O'Leary, Rosemary Gordon, Erika Mantz, and Mike Mangan. My colleagues in the publishing industry also went above and beyond the call of duty. Thanks so much to Tesilya Hanauer, Carole Honeychurch, and Earlita Chenault for their many helpful comments and suggestions. They added a lot to this book.

Any writer knows that writing can be a lonely process and is much more difficult without supportive friends. I've been fortunate to have several friends who spurred me on during various parts of my journey. Many thanks to Maria Tock, Cathy Genna, Nancy Mohrbacher, and Bob Jeffers. I couldn't have done it without them.

My Life Group at New Life Fellowship provided much-needed support at various points along the way, including praying for my poor tired brain on a regular basis. Many thanks to Bob and Margaret Jeffers, Bob and Mary Beth Magan, and Heather and Patrick Martin.

Living with someone who is writing a book is never an easy thing, so my family deserves a special thanks. My husband Doug wears many hats as the spouse of a writer: muse, first reader, proofreader, and sounding board. I can't imagine doing this without him. My sons Ken and Chris also help out in so many ways: finding reference books, helping me pack for conferences, and making me laugh. I thank them for keeping my journey through life so interesting and fun.

How to WRITE *for a* GENERAL AUDIENCE

Introduction

Every year I work editorially with professionals with master's degrees or doctorates who believe that they are writing for the general public. Yet, their use of language includes multi-syllabic words, high diction, and an excess of to-be verbs. I've coined a phrase to describe their problem: "higher educationally impaired."
—*Elizabeth Lyon (2003, p. 19)*

Writing is an essential part of the academic life, but something we often do badly. Generally speaking, we've learned to communicate with a small group of like-minded peers and no one else. One colleague recommends his book to people who can't sleep! Why write things that only the sleep-deprived will endure? How sad is that? And what a waste!

My Writing Journey

I never set out to be a writer or to write for a general audience. For the past 23 years, I've been heavily involved in women's health research. It is my passion. But somewhere along the way, I found that I needed to communicate with a broader audience. My journey began when I worked as a research assistant at Stanford University on a multisite study of premature babies. Writing was about 80% of my job. I knew I needed to write better, so I signed up for some staff development writing courses—one of the best things I ever did. These classes not only made my work easier to do. They also changed my life.

My first foray into writing for a general audience was a hideous little article entitled "How a Baby's Cognitive Development Can Influence Breastfeeding." (This article is not available anywhere, so don't bother looking for it.) I got the idea from questions mothers were asking me. Just when things were going well, their babies' behaviors would change, and it felt like they were back at square one. Naturally, the moms were frustrated. I was sitting there with a PhD in developmental psychology, and it was obvious to me what was going on (e.g., why at 9 months of age, a baby suddenly wouldn't let mom out of his sight). It was my first attempt at finding my general-audience "voice." The article was not very elegant and a little embarrassing. But once I had written it, the next one was easier.

Since then, I've written more than 50 articles and authored or edited 15 books. Five of these books were for a general audience. I've also edited a number of academic books, including a recent 1,000-page tome on intimate partner violence, giving me lots of experience working with academic writers. In 2005, I had 6 books come out—a bit of insanity I never (ever!) plan to repeat. I'll tell you more about these projects as we go along.

HOW TO IMPROVE YOUR WRITING

Your writing journey may be similar to mine. You may have had years of English classes with precious little practical instruction on how to write. The lack of practical instruction most likely continued in graduate school. And then there is that warm and nurturing experience known as peer review, which continues to punish you throughout your career.

Rather than help you, these experiences more likely made writing aversive: something you did because you had to. Even if you wanted to improve, you probably didn't know where to begin. If this describes you, then you've come to the right place. You can learn to write better, and that will open up a whole world of possibilities for you.

If you write in the typical academic style, chances are it's not your fault. Author and editor Theodore Cheney (2005) noted that bad writing tends to be passed from teacher to student, perpetuating the cycle of boring prose. Novelist William Tapply (2005a) made a similar observation. He stated that writing teachers may have encouraged you to write in a way that sounds "smart" but results in poor writing. Some examples include showing off a big vocabulary; writing long, complicated sentences; and filling up lots of pages when fewer would suffice—in short, the academic style:

> Your teachers, I'm afraid, had it all backward. Big words, figures of speech, literary devices and long dense sentences are never admirable for their own sake. Unless used sparely, and always in the service of the story, they just call attention to themselves—and to the writer. . . . Most writers who flaunt their brilliance fall flat on their faces. (Tapply, 2005a, p. 22)

If your previous writing experiences have been bad, you can now put this negative past behind you. As someone who reviews for (at last count) 21 different journals, I can tell you that improving your writing will earn you the love and gratitude of reviewers everywhere. They may not like what you say, but that's another issue. At least you won't be burying your brilliance in a pile of rubble. Therefore, we'll review some of the common mistakes academic writers make that give us our well-deserved "windbag" reputation. Fortunately, these problems are relatively easy to fix, and in chapter 3, I'll show you how.

WHY WRITE?

I will make you a bold promise: Improving your writing will allow you to have fun, make money, and change the world. So let's get started.

Have Fun

There is something almost magical about the written word. In one combination, words can be dull, heavy, and ponderous. With revision, these same words can dance across the page. Bentley (2005) referred to the "alchemy that occurs when the written word collides with the chemicals of your consciousness. Delight is the fruit of that collision" (p. 38).

Your words can enlighten, entertain, and educate. Writing allows you to use your creative abilities and gives you a chance to play with your words. Earlier this year, I was writing a chapter for a book I was editing. My coauthor and I started with typical academic prose. As we worked, we stripped away the excess and were left with clear and compelling text: text that said something. Our words now had fresh air and sunshine. It was exhilarating.

Rather than a necessary evil, writing can become something you look forward to. It is interesting that a surprising number of authors compare writing to sex. For example, author Paul Dickson said that writing is "possibly the most fun you can have with your clothes on" (quoted in Rubie, 2003, p. 6). Writing professor Heather Sellers (2005) made a similar claim: "To create a writing life, you will need to fall in love—deeply, seductively, passionately—with your writing life. It will become not a habit or a job, but a lover" (p. 27). I don't know you, but I'd be willing to bet that you *don't* feel like that about journal articles. And wouldn't it be fun to feel like that? Aren't you at least a little bit curious?

In fairness, I should let you know that writing is not all play; it can be some of the hardest work you'll ever do. But I have a feeling you already know that. Most serious writers work hard at it. Freelance writer John Clausen (2001) opened his book, *Too Lazy to Work, Too Nervous to Steal*, by comparing writing to bull riding:

> True, it's unlikely that you're going to have a murderous, one-ton bovine standing on your chest while you're knocking out a few paragraphs. . . . Big hats, pointy boots . . . and gratuitous physical pain notwithstanding, there are definite similarities in the two jobs. (p. 1)

William Zinsser's (1985) classic work, *On Writing Well*, contains some of the best advice available on writing nonfiction and is one of my favorites. It also contains many pages of kvetching about how difficult it is to write clear prose. So don't be surprised or discouraged by how challenging writing can be. It's part of the process. But as your writing improves, you'll have the most amazing sense of satisfaction. And one day, it will suddenly occur to you that writing is also fun.

Make Money

Writing for money is often a novel concept for academics; most of the writing that we do is for free or for relatively small sums of money. But writing can generate income. You may not start out by making much. As you gain experience, however, you can charge— and get—higher fees for your work.

Granted, most of you probably won't get rich from writing. But the potential is there, especially if you become a "crossover" author and branch out into general-audience publications (Clausen, 2001). Let me give you an example. For a general-audience book, you may make about $1.00 per copy in royalties. If you've written an academic book, your royalty payment per book is likely to be higher, but you'll sell a lot fewer of them. The average nonfiction book sells about 7,500 copies (see, e.g., Poynter, 2004). However, one of your titles may do even better. Let's say that your book sells 100,000 copies. You do the math. Writing may become so lucrative and satisfying that you decide to do it full time.

Another way that writing can impact your bottom line is through parallel work. Writing for a general audience can lead to speaking engagements—and these can pay quite well. Even if your fee for speaking is small, which it may be when you first start out, you often have the opportunity to sell your books directly. The combination of royalties and direct sales can mean thousands of dollars each year.

But money and fun are only two of the reasons for writing. This next one is even more important.

Change the World and Rediscover Your Passion

The winter of 1776–1777 was bleak for the newly formed Continental Army: They were out of money. The troops had inadequate gear. Many did not have footwear, causing them to leave bloody footprints in the snow. The soldiers were ragged and starving, and there was little General Washington could do to ease their suffering. What made the difference? Words. That's right, words.

Thomas Paine, serving as the aide-de-camp to General Nathaniel Greene, penned these famous words in one of a series of essays known as *The Crisis*. Paine wrote *The Crisis* because he was "sick at heart" with the suffering he saw all around him. His "passion of patriotism" (McCullough, 2005, p. 251) prompted him to write for the sole purpose of rallying people's flagging spirits to the cause:

> These are the times that try men's souls. The summer soldier and the sunshine patriot will, in this crisis, shrink from the service of his country; but he that stands it now, deserves the love and thanks of man and woman. Tyranny, like hell, is not easily conquered; yet we have this consolation with us, that the harder the conflict, the more glorious the triumph. What we obtain too cheap, we esteem too lightly; it is dearness only that gives everything its value. Heaven knows how to put a proper price upon its goods; and it would be strange indeed if so celestial an article as FREEDOM should not be highly rated. (Paine, 1776/2004, p. 49)

Thomas Paine couldn't give the soldiers material goods. But he provided them the strength to carry on another day. After I had already drafted this section of the book you are reading, I took my kids to Valley Forge and found, to my interest, that the National Park Service's display specifically mentions the impact of these words on the American forces with the following notation: "Thomas Paine publishes The Crisis, which helps rekindle the fires of liberty during the darkest hours of the Revolution."

Despots too know the power of words. That's why anyone trying to control a population first targets the press (Rubie, 2003). Even the infamous Stamp Act, which preceded the American Revolution, was an attempt to control the press and their publication of seditious tracts. The power of words is why a free press is essential to a free society.

The power of the written word has not faded, even in this electronic age (Smokler, 2005). *America's Right Turn* (Viguerie & Franke, 2004), *Blog* (Hewitt, 2005), and *The Grassfire Effect* (Elliot, 2005) are three recent books that describe how alternative media shaped the political and cultural landscape. What do these books have in common? All three extol the power of writing:

> All say that, no matter how flashy the effects, in the end it's all about story. . . . We writers are the frontline artisans of story. It's our world out there, no matter how humble and plain our creations seem in comparison. (Smokler, 2005, p. 11)

Australian freelance writer Michael Meanwell (2004) made a similar point:

> One of the key discoveries by smart Web entrepreneurs is that content is king. . . . In fact, surveys have shown that the most effective Web sites in terms of hits or sales are those that focus less on design and more on content, particularly the clear presentation of information. (p. 57)

Can your words change the world? Absolutely! Let's face it. Most of us got into our fields because we were passionate about our subjects. We wanted our knowledge to make a difference. But practicalities got in the way. We had meetings to attend, classes to teach, journal articles to write. So our dreams of impacting others got deferred or written off as not realistic. The exciting thing is that by writing, you can revive those dreams and use your hard-won education to make a difference for others.

Your words may never inspire mass political movements. But they can still influence people in your field and beyond. Thomas Hale, a pharmacologist and professor of pediatrics at Texas Tech University Medical School, has had a large impact in the field of perinatal health. He became very skilled at listening to what his audience needed to know about pharmacology and communicating that information in an understandable way. His ability to communicate clearly has influenced health care practice all over the world. I'll tell you more about his work in chapter 9.

It may take a while for your words to have an effect. You may need time to master your craft and learn the ropes of publication. But I believe this kind of impact is within your grasp. For those of you who persevere, the rewards are many.

Besides offering information, writing can also give your readers a glimpse of the sublime. In a world of ugliness, words can convey a sense of transcendent beauty. Writer Anne Lamott (1994) expressed it this way:

> Think of those times when you've read prose or poetry that is presented in such a way that you have a fleeting glimpse of being startled by beauty or insight, by a glimpse into someone's soul. ... This is our goal as writers, I think; to help others have this sense of ... wonder, or seeing things anew, that can catch us off guard, that breaks in on our small, bordered worlds. (pp. 99–100)

What You Can Expect From This Book

You may have picked up this book because you want to write better. Perhaps you are toying with the idea of reaching a broader audience. You may want to write a book but have no idea where to begin. Or you may just want to see what's out there in terms of opportunities. In any of these cases, this book can help.

In talking with colleagues, I've found that many lack knowledge about how publications work. Therefore, I want to take you through the business end of publishing. So often, academic writers make avoidable mistakes because they don't know how the process works. I want to help you to be your most effective.

Chapters 1 through 7 of this book provide an overview of the process of writing, where I describe the actual writing and editing. I'll show you some common mistakes that academic authors make and how to fix them. I'll also introduce you to some new styles of writing that will give you additional tools for making yourself heard. We'll also talk about some time-management techniques to help you use your writing time well and to enlist things like procrastination in working for, rather than against, you. Finally, I'll teach you how to be a writer whom editors love.

In chapters 8 through 13, I describe the range of writing you can do. I'll take you through writing articles for a general audience. You'll learn how to query magazine editors and learn what they need from you. If you've been thinking about writing a book, I'll walk you through that process as well. We'll review some of the insider's language from the publishing industry. I'll demystify queries and book proposals, describe book contracts, and give you at least a rudimentary knowledge of copyright law. I'll also talk to you about book promotion and marketing, and what those ranking numbers on Amazon.com mean.

For the examples used in this book, I drew from the literature on childbirth and women's issues because this is my specialty area and the one in which I have published the most. Readers will want to draw on their own preferred themes and special knowledge for writing material.

I hope that the personal experiences I relate in this book will help you avoid some common pitfalls and become a successful crossover author. I have deliberately focused primarily on approaching smaller specialty publishers because I believe that novice writers are more likely to be successful in approaching editors at these companies. I also focus on getting published in magazines and trade publications because these outlets give beginning crossover writers a chance to build up a portfolio of articles and publishing credits that they can then show to book publishers.

In short, this book shares with you the tricks of the trade that I have learned, mostly by trial and error and via helpful mentors along the way. I want your work to succeed, and I want you to avoid making mistakes that can scuttle your success and give us all a bad reputation at the same time. So join me as I guide you through this fascinating, and sometimes frustrating, process. I think you'll enjoy the journey. See you in print!

1

Getting Started:
From Idea to First Draft

Almost all good writing begins with terrible first efforts.
You need to start somewhere. Start by getting
something—anything—down on paper.
—Anne Lamott (1994, p. 25)

For most writers, getting started is the hardest part. Whether you are writing a paragraph or a book, it all begins with getting those first words down on paper. And that's the focus of this chapter. I'll describe some ways to stop messing around, get past your inner critic, and produce a first draft. But first things first: You need a good idea.

COMING UP WITH A GREAT IDEA

Ideas can come from anywhere. You may be watching television and see something that really annoys you or that you know is just not true. That spark can lead to an article or even a book. You can get ideas from talking with others. They can help you to identify a need for information or advice, or one idea may lead to a completely different project.

When I wrote *The Hidden Feelings of Motherhood*, a book about mothering stress (Kendall-Tackett, 2001, 2005c), I included a chapter on housework. I wrote that chapter to acknowledge that housework is a huge source of stress in families and shared some techniques to make it a little easier. I thought these techniques were pretty straightforward. As it turned out, they were less obvious than I thought. After *Hidden Feelings* was published, people told me that they loved the housework chapter. The reaction I received was the first kernel of an idea for another book, *The Well-Ordered Home* (Kendall-Tackett, 2003). I never set out to write a book on household organization. But suddenly it seemed like a possibility.

Reading in the genre in which you want to write can also be an important source of ideas. If you read, then ideas will come. One writing teacher recommended that her students become "promiscuous" readers (Sellers, 2005). If you are not already doing so, start reading widely in fields outside your immediate area of interest. You'll be amazed at the number of ideas you generate.

The Idea File

When inspiration hits, jot your ideas down as soon as possible. Ideas will often come when you least expect them: in the shower; while driving or chopping vegetables; or most annoying, when you are just dropping off to sleep. The unconscious mind generally will not work on demand and is slowed significantly when you force things. So when good or even so-so ideas bubble to the surface, write them down. If you don't, I can pretty much guarantee that when it's time to write, you'll be fresh out of ideas and your precious writing time will go to waste. In contrast, if you have a list of ideas, whenever you do have a bit of time you will be ready to leap into action. Isn't that better than staring at a blank computer screen?

Once you jot your ideas down, put your notes in a single place. This will become your *idea file*. As ideas form, you may want to start a separate file for each project. Your idea file can be electronic or hard copy (or both). As you think of other things you want to include, jot those ideas down and put them in the file. If you find a journal or magazine article that applies to that project, throw it in the file. For me, sometimes weeks or months pass before I get to that file. But when I'm ready to write, I have everything assembled.

Write What You Know

Another source of inspiration can be conveying what you already know to a larger audience. What do readers need to know about your topic? What's new in the field? Often, you may start with a specific publication in mind.

Ideas can also come because you love your topic. Surgeon Atul Gawande, in his book *Complications*

(Gawande, 2002), related stories about his various adventures in medicine. In one chapter, he described a patient so morbidly obese that he could not go to a ball game or the movies. He chronicled what happened to this man after gastric bypass surgery. In another chapter, he described how, against all the obvious evidence, a patient of his was infected with necrotizing fasciitis (so-called "flesh-eating bacteria"). He stated that medicine often comes down to making intuitive judgments that go against the evidence. In this case, nothing on the surface indicated that his patient had this condition. But "something" made him perform a biopsy that identified this condition and saved his patient's life.

Ideas for articles or books do not need to be from your field. Often, a fruitful source of ideas is your hobby or passion rather than your vocation. Mike Mangan, a psychology professor at the University of New Hampshire, has written a book about surf etiquette. This book grew out of 25 years of experience as a surfer and his desire to educate people who are new to the sport (see chap. 9). An attorney I know is an avid bodybuilder, so he writes about bodybuilding. You may be a professor in one field, but your passion is wine, model aircraft, Boy Scouts, or stamp collecting. You could write about these subjects or anything else you feel passionately about.

Not every idea that flits across your brain is going to work as an article or book. But don't censor yourself at this stage, when the idea first occurs to you. We often kill some potentially good ideas by being too critical. So jot the idea down and allow your mind some time to chew on it. As you do, you'll move into the next phase: refining and focusing your idea.

In the refining stage, you start thinking through the practicalities of your idea. What form do you see it taking? Article, blog, book? Or something else? Whom do you consider the audience for this idea? How could you get it to them? The purpose of this phase is to help you narrow your focus and see if you could write something on the topic you are considering. But don't overthink things even at this stage. Sometimes you just need to sit down and write it until you have an idea about whether it's going to work.

Generally speaking, it's helpful if you have an idea about the market you are trying to reach. But this is not a hard-and-fast rule. I sometimes write things without having a clear sense of where it will go when it's finished. I just need to write to help me think through the idea. These types of articles and books may be more difficult to place (because you aren't writing with a particular set of specs in mind). But if the piece is well written and has helpful information, you can probably find a home for it. I once had an idea for an article on postpartum rituals in other countries and how these seemed to protect mothers from postpartum depression (i.e., rituals that "mothered the new mother"). I wrote that article without any thought of where it would go. Eventually, it was published in three different publications and became part of one of my books.

WRITING A FIRST DRAFT

Now for the hard part. Once you've landed on a great idea, it's time to start getting words down on paper. The first draft stops many an aspiring writer right in his or her tracks. You may be bursting with good ideas, but somehow, what comes out on paper is . . . horrible. Because of this disconnect, it's easy to put things off, procrastinate, and not get around to writing anything.

Get Out of Your Own Way: That Little Voice Inside Your Head

One reason why it's often hard to start is because of that little voice inside our heads. Even when we have time and something interesting to say, our minds keep us from moving past the first paragraph. This is the voice that tells you that your writing is awful, that you really should give up, that you have no talent, and that you'll never get better. Talk with other writers, and you'll find out what a common experience this is. Freelance writer Jacqueline Fletcher (2005) described it this way: "Every writer knows that having an inner censor—that little voice that tells you to give up, you're no good, you'll never be a 'real' writer—is part of the writing life" (p. 36). Novelist Michele Bardsley (2005) told a similar tale as she recounted the phone call that told her that she had won the grand prize in the *Writer's Digest* writing competition:

> Editor: Is this Michele Bardsley?
> Michele: Yes.
> *Oh crap. Something happened to my entry. It got shredded. It got wet. It got set on fire.*
> Editor: Hang on.
> *They hated my story and called to tell me to never, ever enter again.*
> Editor: OK, here it is.
> *I suck. I suck. I suck.*
> Editor: You've won the grand prize. Congratulations!
> Michele: Huh? (p. 31)

Heather Sellers has told aspiring writers that if they want to write, they must "dare to suck" (Sellers, 2005, p. 109). Most writers are bad at the beginning—especially when trying a new genre or different type of writing. Writing cruddy first drafts can be challenging for academics because they have already attained a certain level of prestige and professional competence. It's hard on the ego to be bad at something. But once you get through this stage, you'll find that it becomes much easier.

One more thing: Try to avoid drawing false conclusions about your writing on the basis of comparisons with others. Here's why I say that. In my younger days, I trained for many years as a musician. Because of that, I know how much effort goes into making a final performance appear effortless. It takes hours and hours of scales, mistakes, and taking things at half speed.

Keep that in mind when you compare your writing—especially your first drafts—with someone else's finished prose. They most likely went through many drafts to get to the final form. So it is absurd to compare your unedited text with someone else's final version and then conclude that you can't write. What appears effortless to you as a reader was most likely the result of a lot of effort. Or as John Clausen (2001) said, "There is no such thing as 'good writing.' There is only good rewriting" (p. 138).

The Role of Cognitive Distortions

Mental health professionals describe the negative thoughts that plague writers as *cognitive distortions*. In cognitive therapy, the way to address cognitive distortions is to first recognize them and then ask yourself whether they are true. David Burns, the psychiatrist who popularized cognitive therapy, has described how he was afflicted with doubt before he wrote his second book. His first book, *Feeling Good* (Burns, 1980), had sold millions. His editor wanted him to write another book and predicted that this book too would be a best seller. Burns became completely paralyzed with doubt and didn't feel he could write "another best seller." For a while, he could not write at all. It was only when he gave himself permission to write something that wasn't a best seller that he could write *The Feeling Good Handbook* (1990).

I've gone through a similar process with almost all of my books. When I'm working on a book proposal and going back and forth with an editor, I'm confident that I can do the job. I'm excited about getting started. I know it's going to be good.

Then I get the contract. Once that happens, I have my postcontract panic attack. I become convinced that I don't know anything about the subject, that I won't be able to write more than five pages about it, and that everyone else could do a better job. These beliefs paralyze me.

It is interesting that it was with my book *The Well-Ordered Home* (Kendall-Tackett, 2003) when I especially felt this. This book has sold better than any of my other books. Yet I was completely frozen for the first few weeks, unable to write a thing. A lot of that paralysis came from the silly things I thought needed to be true for me to write that book, and some of these misbeliefs came from my interactions with others. For example, when I told people about my contract, I had several people say that *they* should write the book—not me—because they were much more organized and so forth (it was probably true!). I also got static from some of my academic friends who couldn't believe that I—academic-researcher girl—was writing a book on household organization. The topic of housework did not have the serious tone that they thought appropriate. On top of everything, I was exhausting myself trying to be perfectly organized all the time. How could

I write about this topic if my house wasn't always perfect?

These ridiculous thoughts completely stopped me. By recognizing them, I was able to challenge them with the truth and finally knuckle down and write the book. First, it dawned on me that my book was in no way keeping others from writing a similar book. The reason I was writing the book, and not them, was because I was the one who wrote a book proposal and got a contract. If my well-organized friends wanted to write one, then they certainly could. That recognition took away the irrational guilt I was feeling.

The Well-Ordered Home certainly doesn't embody academic seriousness. But I can live with that. I recognized that this book could actually be helpful to people who read it. As I mentioned earlier, household tasks are a huge source of stress for families. By making tasks easier, organization could improve people's lives.

Finally, I had to let go of my anxiety about not having a perfect house. In fact, it was David Burns, in his book that he was worried would not be a best seller, who gave me the way out. I don't have to be perfect! I realized that audiences would probably be able to identify with me better if I wasn't perfect. So, in the book, I told readers that I am not naturally organized; that left to my own devices, I lean more toward chaos—that my own mother couldn't believe that I'd written a book on household organization. Once I could admit all these things, I was free to write the book.

Having had at least a dozen postcontract panic attacks, I can tell you that they are getting shorter and shorter. I can now point to a stack of completed books and realize that I had panic attacks with each of them and that what I worried about did not come to pass. I was able to write more than five pages. I actually did know what I was talking about. And yes, there were people outside of my immediate family who were interested in what I had to say.

How to Deal With Your Inner Critic

There are various ways you can deal with your inner critic. In classic cognitive therapy fashion, you could either explicitly write out your fears and concerns or tell them to a confidant. Often, the act of voicing these concerns or seeing them in black and white can go a long way to help you recognize their irrationality. Friends and relatives can also be helpful.

One classic type of cognitive distortion that is common among writers is all-or-nothing thinking. All-or-nothing thinking tends to result in the use of "always" and "never," as in, "I'll never get this published. I'm such a lousy writer, I'll never improve. I always procrastinate on projects and can never get them done." Sound familiar? If you find yourself thinking this way, challenge those thoughts with the truth. For example, is it really true that you will *never* improve? What about what you are writing right now? Isn't it better than what you used to do? Don't you deserve some credit for trying to learn something new—at your age? And why do you think you have to do this perfectly right from the start?

If you want to know more about cognitive distortions and how to deal with them, I'd encourage you to pick up Burns's two books I referenced earlier. *The Feeling Good Handbook* (1990), particularly, has quite a bit to say about his process as a writer. I think you'll find these books both helpful and encouraging.

Fletcher (2005) described how more concrete tools can also be helpful. In her case, she pictures her inner critic as Gollum from *The Lord of the Rings*. She bought herself a toy Gollum that says "my precious" when she pushes the button. Once she hears this, she laughs and can get back to work. One of her friends embodies her critic as a Barbie doll. Whenever these voices get the better of her, she tosses the Barbie into the trash can next to her desk. Then she gets back to work. The techniques may seem a little corny, but if you think they would work for you, why not give them a try? (I promise not to tell!)

There are two take-away messages here:

- Most writers are afflicted with doubts about their writing abilities at some point in the process. Success doesn't make these go away, but it can make them more intense if writers are convinced that they can't live up to their past greatness.
- By recognizing this inner voice, you can work past it and go on to write something wonderful. Re-

member, it doesn't have to be perfect to be good. Give yourself permission to be a learner again. Your writing will be the better for it.

The Importance of Downtime

One reason writers may find themselves blocked is that they work all the time. This can be an especially challenging problem for academics, who tend to work long hours already. Your mind needs time to play. And although you can probably force prose by plodding along, what you write will be missing that spark of inspiration and will be much harder to create.

When you have downtime, your brain is free to roam, make connections, and experiment with wording. Many writers talk about what happens when they sleep on an idea. Something they just couldn't solve the day before suddenly seems clear. John Clausen (2001) also found that when his mind was well-rested, he came up with better ideas. It is during downtime that those serendipitous connections happen—and those connections can be really amazing.

Another source of inspiration might seem strange at first, but I've heard enough authors talk about it to know that it's helpful: the simple joy of the mindless, repetitive task. I've always noticed how great ideas occur to me while I am painting, doing needlework, or cleaning. It's really helpful to do something physical that doesn't require a great deal of thought. I remember reading that one author used to balance his writing time with yard work. He found that combining these two activities helped his creative process. When he hit a snag in his writing, he'd grab his hedge shears and head for the yard. My only caution is to recognize when your "downtime" becomes a way to procrastinate. When it does, it's time to quit the mindless task.

Don't Fight Your Natural Thinking Style

Someone once described me as a *linear thinker*. I had no idea what she was talking about, but as I later explained to my mom, I was pretty sure it wasn't a compliment. Several months later, I happened to read a book that described linear thinkers (McGee-Cooper, 1994). They are ones who basically think in logical order: Point A leads to Point B that leads to Point C. I definitely am not one of those.

McGee-Cooper (1994) contrasted this with the *divergent thinker*. This is someone who starts working on one topic, then gets an idea for something else, which leads to yet another thing. That is definitely me. I've known for a long time that I'm likely to bounce around when I'm writing. I'll be working on chapter 8 when I suddenly have a great idea for chapter 2. When I'm working on a big project, like a book, it's not unusual for me to have several chapters open at once. My brother-in-law, a commercial artist, has a similar working style. He tends to work on three or four paintings at a time. His process for painting is quite similar to mine for writing.

When I recognized my thinking style and stopped fighting it, I was a lot more productive, and this might be true for you, too. You can get really bogged down if you try to limit yourself to the way you "should" write. Often, we start at the beginning and expect to write straight through. Some people can certainly do this. But if you don't work this way, then don't assume you have to change. If you want to start in the middle or end, then that's okay. The best way for you to write is the way that works for you.

How About an Outline?

Opinion is mixed on whether an outline is necessary. I generally need to write first before I can produce a comprehensive outline. If I had to write an outline first, I'd probably get stuck. The act of writing in and of itself helps me think through what needs to be in an article or book. That being said, I usually need a rough idea of where I am going. So I am likely to jot notes about the general points I want to cover. Once I have something drafted, I'm likely to move things around, but it is helpful to start with at least a rudimentary road map.

Sometimes, I have no idea about how the pieces will fit together. In those cases, I will often brainstorm on a piece of paper about all the things I want to include. I don't worry about how these will fit together at this point. I may write the topics down all over the page. Once I have this rough listing of what I want to include, it is much easier for me to put the ideas into a meaningful sequence.

The main thing you want to avoid is getting stalled in the process. Write as much as you can without getting hung up on the particulars. Sometimes, just the process of writing can help you think through the logical order of what you want to say.

Conclusion

Beginnings are often the most difficult part of writing. Our culture's incessant busyness may block your ability to think clearly or come up with good ideas. It can also be challenging to get past your inner critic who makes negative comments about anything you do put down on paper. Fortunately, there are ways you can work around these obstacles. Just remember that most writers write rotten first drafts, and give yourself permission to not show them to anyone; they do not reflect what you can really do but are only the first step.

2

Finding Time to Write:
Time Management for Writers

*Writing is a ton of work. It's exhausting. . . . It's like
cleaning house—fun to have finished, less fun to do.*
—Heather Sellers (2005, p. 65)

All writers struggle, at some point in their careers,
with finding time to write. In this chapter, I present
a range of strategies that working authors use to fit
writing in with the rest of their lives. These techniques
are highly individual. What works for you may not
work for your friend, and vice versa. Chances are,
however, that at least one of these techniques will
help. And the more strategies you have, the more
likely you are to succeed.

SET ASIDE TIME TO WRITE

Writing takes time. I state the obvious because begin-
ning authors often forget to allocate time for writing.
Some projects, like a book, can take a year or longer.
Are you at a place in your life where you can take

that kind of time? It's a question you should seriously consider.

Much of finding time to write comes down to setting priorities. If writing has a high priority in your life, then it needs to come before other things. Sellers (2005) described how a friend of hers sets aside time to write in the same way that she trains for a marathon. When writing, she describes herself as "in training" and says no to other things. She refuses to do errands, comes late to social events or blows them off entirely if she is on a roll, and declines a lot of other obligations. It may not be necessary to do all of that in order to write. But her point is well taken: Choosing to write means you'll have to refuse or at least delay some other things in your life.

In a classic demonstration, author and management guru Stephen Covey (2004) has described how prioritizing our work can influence what we are able to accomplish. He demonstrated with two beakers that he would eventually fill with rocks, sand, gravel, and water. In the first container, he added the gravel and sand first, leaving no room for the big rocks. In the second container, when he added the big rocks first, the sand, gravel, and water still fit, working their way around the big rocks.

He then applied this principle to time and life management. The big rocks represent the major things that you want to accomplish in your day, week, year, or life. When you see to those big-rock items first, all of the other urgent but less important things fit in around the big rocks. In contrast, when we let our lives be run by smaller urgent things, we may never get around to the important big-rock things we want to do. If writing is something you want to do, then it needs to be a big rock in your life.

Sometimes, circumstances in people's lives are such that they really don't have time to write. I recently met someone who apologized to me that she had "only" published two books. This woman had a full-time clinical practice and a full speaking schedule. And she was working on her PhD. I couldn't believe that she was apologizing! Another woman told me she wished she could do more writing. As we chatted, I asked her how many children she had—nine, all boys. I had to excuse myself and go lie down. How realistic would it have been for either of these women to write?

That being said, sometimes writing becomes a lifeline in times of difficulty—so squeezing it in is a good idea. Stephen King, in *On Writing* (King, 2000), described his long recovery from a serious accident, in which he was hit by a truck as he walked along a country road. During this recovery, King fell into a deep depression. In his book, he described how writing became his creative outlet and his vision of life beyond being injured. It became an important part of his recovery.

Similarly, Stephen Ambrose wrote his last book, *To America* (Ambrose, 2002), while battling lung cancer. In the acknowledgments section, Ambrose thanked his doctor, who had suggested that he write as part of his recovery. His last book was a fascinating behind-the-scenes glimpse into how he had written his other books. Although he did not survive his cancer, writing seems to have kept him from despairing over his condition and engaged with life until the end.

My point is that it is not always possible to tell from outside circumstances whether someone has time to write. You may be a person who by all outward appearances has no time to write. And you may decide to postpone writing until life is a little more sane. Or you may decide that even 15 minutes a day will keep you sane. This is a decision only you can make.

DOES IT HELP TO HAVE A CONTRACT?

A lot of people ask me whether I get a contract before I start writing. I always do. But this is a personal decision. Sociologist David Finkelhor, who has published 11 books, prefers not to have a contract ahead of time. He likes to do the work and then shop for a publisher. Obviously, either strategy works. But getting a contract after you have finished a book may be difficult for a beginning writer and only possible once you have a track record.

I've put this topic in the time-management chapter because it is relevant to how I budget my own time. It would be much more difficult for me to take the time necessary to write a book if I didn't know it was going somewhere when it was finished. Deadlines are also helpful to me. Otherwise, work falls into the abyss of writing projects labeled "someday." Whatever approach you decide to take, it's important to do what works for you.

Minimize Procrastination

If you were to survey authors about their writing challenges, most would place procrastination at or near the top of the list. Writing is a lonely process and a lot of hard work, and it's amazing all the things that authors will do to avoid getting started. They get a drink, go to the bathroom, or check e-mail. They sharpen all of their pencils, clean out their desk drawer, or decide to catch up on those journals stacking up on their desks. They run an urgent errand, make a call, or order something online. Is any of this ringing a bell?

Procrastination can be a problem throughout the writing process. When authors don't have time, they often long for "time to write." Yet when there is time, all of a sudden there are 20 other things to do. Even experienced authors with lots of publications to their credit can be black-belt procrastinators. To minimize your procrastination time, I've provided some strategies that can help.

Give Yourself a Set Time to Work

Authors often dread starting because the task before them appears endless. And who wants to work on an endless task? To counter that feeling of dread, one effective technique is to give yourself a set time to work. Fifteen minutes is a good amount. Surely, you can spare 15 minutes. If you need to, set a timer. When the 15 minutes are up, you can stop, or you may decide to keep working. Either way, you've got something to show for your time. And I think you will be amazed at what you can accomplish in that amount of time. When you know you only have a short time, you'll probably be more focused and actually get more done than in an unfocused hour.

Use Procrastination

When you really dread doing something, sometimes you can use that feeling to get started on another project that you've also been dreading but maybe dreading a little less. I've been doing this for years. It's one of the great advantages of having several projects going at once: I can use them to bounce off of each other.

I became consciously aware of this technique last spring, when I was teaching research methods. I took a teaching assignment for the spring semester at the last minute, to help someone out of a jam. In the meantime, I had to turn in a book manuscript on May 1. It was not great planning on my part.

As part of the class, my students worked on research proposals. The first section of the proposal was their literature reviews. As I expected, most of the reviews were dreadful. I mean, really dreadful. It took me a full week to grade them because there was just so much to mark. (And the students had the chance to turn them in again.) When they turned in their Method sections, I wasn't exactly aching to get to work on them. Suddenly, I couldn't wait to work on my manuscript. I would tell myself, "I'll just work on one chapter. . . ." And pretty soon, one led to another, and another. Before I knew it, I had taken a first pass through two thirds of the book. Procrastinating on my grading was suddenly a great incentive to work on a revision on which I was also procrastinating.

My only caution in using procrastination is that you need to keep track of your deadlines. Don't procrastinate so much that you miss an important deadline. But you may find that this technique gives you just the energy you need to break your procrastination cycle.

Make Your Work Easy to Do

This is another technique I discovered by accident. I came to my postdoc with a small stash of articles in various stages of completion. I had each article in a separate folder that contained any drafts, notes, and data analysis that I needed. During that year, I also had some significant health problems and spent a lot of time at the doctor's office. I wrote most of my articles while sitting in waiting rooms. I ended up writing quite a few articles that year, and I was able to do it because I made it easy to write. This technique can help you, too. To increase your writing productivity, get in the habit of taking your writing wherever you go. You'll be amazed at how much you can get done during those odd bits of time.

Shorten Your Warm-Up Time

Another technique is to jot down a few notes about where you want to go next before you quit for the day. Even if you only write down a few words, you will be able to quickly find your place again. Without these cues, it may take a while to get going. And by the time you do, your work time will be almost gone. If you write yourself a brief note, then you'll be able to bypass the long warm-up and get right to work.

Use Brain-Dead Days, Too

We all have days when we're really fuzzy. We might be exhausted because we've been doing too much. Or we've been traveling. Or we have a cold. Whatever the reason, there are days when writing or even serious editing will be too much for our feeble minds to handle. You can sit there and laboriously pound out something for 4 hours that would normally take only 1. Or you can go another way. And that's what I recommend.

On those days, do your tedious writing tasks: Check your references, type your references, or look up material that you need. These tasks have to be done sometime. It's much better to do them ahead of time rather than waiting until your deadline. And your editor will love you because you'll have taken care of those details that most authors miss. Remember, this is writing too! And activities you perform on brain-dead days can also be great warm-ups for other types of writing.

Avoid Black Holes of Time

I hang around with a lot of academics, and almost everyone I know works really hard. But even the most efficient of us have little time wasters slip in and add to an already too-full schedule. Unfortunately, these time wasters can be another way to procrastinate and keep you from writing. I call them "black holes of time." In a typical day, people can easily waste an hour or more because they've stumbled into a black hole. Fortunately, there is something you can do. Start by becoming aware of the activities that keep you from writing.

E-Mail

For many of you, e-mail is writing enemy Number 1. The tyranny of e-mail is something that professional organizer Julie Morgenstern addressed in *Making Work Work* (Morgenstern, 2004). She stated that e-mail dramatically decreases our efficiency and recommended that most of us avoid it for the 1st hour in the morning unless absolutely necessary. This is good advice. Try it, and I think you'll agree. She also recommended batching e-mail so that it doesn't interrupt you throughout the day. Constant interruptions make it much harder to concentrate, and "checking your e-mail" can become a major way to procrastinate. Writing is hard enough without giving yourself an excuse for not doing it.

Computer Games and Cyberslacking

Computer games can also take time away from our writing. For me, computer solitaire is deadly. I removed it from my computer because I couldn't resist it. I'd find myself thinking, "I'll just play one game to 'warm up.'" I think you know what happened next.

Similarly, surfing the Internet can eat up hours of time. This is so common in the workplace that there is a new term for it: *cyberslacking*. For writers, cyberslacking can take the form of "research." Yes, you probably do need to do research. The trick is to know when it's time to stop and apply what you have learned. If you find that you are endlessly researching and never writing, then start setting some concrete writing goals for yourself. If necessary, enlist help from a colleague or friend to keep you accountable.

Office Chitchat

Office chitchat can also be a black hole. Yes, it's necessary to talk with your colleagues. But if you find that you are getting little done, you'll want to limit these interactions as well. One strategy I suggest is being direct with people who keep hanging around your work space ("I have to get back to work. I need to turn this in at 2."). You can also go someplace else. Find a quiet conference room, preferably on another floor. If you work on a campus, go to the library. Or work from home. Being away from your normal work space can help you get started and keep you focused and productive.

Perfectionism

Author Anne Lamott (1994) described perfectionism as the "voice of the oppressor" (p. 28) and said that you will not get much writing done until you get over it. As an editor, I see this all the time. I meet people who want to write, but they can't get past the first paragraph because they think it needs to be "perfect." They keep editing and editing, well past the time when it makes any difference.

Perfectionism can be rooted in your experiences with critical parents. Or you may have developed it through interactions with overly critical writing in-structors. These are folks who manage to suck all the joy from writing and spend a lot of time convincing others that they don't know how to write. If you've had experiences with perfectionistic teachers, then ask yourself whether they do much writing. If they don't, it's time to exorcise them from your consciousness. Even if they do, realize that they may be trying to make everyone else write exactly like them, which is totally unnecessary and is, in fact, a bad idea. Don't try to sound like anyone but yourself.

My advice for avoiding perfectionism is to make your text coherent and eliminate as many typos as you can but realize that there comes a stopping point. What you write doesn't have to be perfect. And even with more editing, it may never be. If you find that you're never getting stuff finished, then it's time to consider why and make some changes in how you approach your work.

Use Rituals

If you hang around with writers for very long, one thing you will notice is that many have little rituals or routines that they follow to help them write. And rituals might help you as well. You may like to use a certain type of pen and paper. Some prolific writers will only use sharp Number 2 pencils and yellow legal pads. A surprising number of working writers still like using typewriters; they like the kinesthetic feel of the keys hitting the page. Put them in front of a computer keyboard and their minds go blank (Scott, 2005). Other writers have certain clothes they like to wear while writing—or not. The late Barbara Cartland, queen of the romance novel, purportedly did most of her writing naked, sitting at her piano (Bentley, 2005). I live in New England. That sounds pretty chilly to me. The list of rituals is endless.

I have certain music that I have designated as my "writing music." When I put those CDs on, I know it's time to write. Lately, my favorite writing music is the soundtrack from the movie *Pirates of the Caribbean*. That may seem an odd choice, but for me it is almost the perfect tempo for typing. Ditto with the movie soundtrack from *Phantom of the Opera*. It's pure stimulus–response: When I hear the opening refrains from these soundtracks, I have an overwhelming urge to write. You might find that certain types of music may help you as well.

Unfortunately, as useful as they are, rituals can be taken too far. I once knew a woman who would don "writing togs" every time she needed to write something longer than a few pages. Her togs were basically scruffy looking clothing (looking, to my eye, like "painting togs" or "cleaning-out-the-garage togs," but I digress). The problem is they didn't seem to help her produce much writing.

Do You Need to Write Every Day?

One ritual that many experienced writers use is to write every day. Stephen King is one example. In *On Writing* (King, 2000), he described how he works every morning to produce 10 pages of text. By drafting 10 pages a day, he is able to be one of the most prolific writers in America. If he produces 50 pages a week, then by 10 weeks he has 500 pages—the average length of one of his novels. Yes, he still has to go back and edit. In fact, that's often where the real work begins. But by getting the words down on paper, he keeps projects moving forward.

Opinion varies widely among instructors about whether writers need to write every day. Some instructors tell students that unless they are writing every day, they are not "real" writers. From my perspective, the advice to write every day is good. When I can do it, I'm superproductive. The problem is that I've never been able to make it work for me long term; my life keeps getting in the way. My schedule is irregular. I travel a lot. There are times when I may not write for weeks. Yet, I'm still productive. One person I know who feels it's necessary to write every day takes 5 years to complete a book. In contrast, I don't write every day, but it takes me about 8 to 9 months to complete a book. And in recent years, I've worked on several at once.

My most effective scheduling happens when I cluster my work. If I have a deadline coming up, I'll put in a lot more hours than if I have nothing immediately pending. I keep track of all of my various deadlines and work accordingly. I also adopt a modified version of Stephen King's approach. I calculate how many weeks I have until a deadline, and then figure out how many pages a week I need to produce to make that deadline. This approach may seem the antithesis of "creative." But even creative types need some structure for their work. If you are falling behind or not getting anything done, having concrete goals might help.

So my conclusion on writing every day is if you can make that work for you, then it's probably good discipline and will make it easier to meet deadlines in a timely fashion. However, if you can't find time to write every day, make sure that you are regularly producing writing, even if it tends to cluster.

In summary, rituals can help you get past the major hurdle of starting to write, and that's a good thing. Rituals will also add to your allure as a writer and might even mark you as a genuine eccentric. However, they cease to be useful when you are spending most of your time participating in the ritual and precious little time writing.

Have a Nice Place to Work

Where you work can also make a difference in how productive you are. Try to make your work space as pleasant as possible. Do you have a comfortable place to sit? Is it a good temperature? Is there enough light? Is your computer or monitor positioned so you don't get eye strain? Your office does not have to be expensively furnished to work well. But you are more likely to spend time there if it's a nice place to be.

Change of Scenery

If you are stuck, sometimes a change of scenery can be just what you need. For some reason, working in restaurants, cafes, or fast-food joints has always worked well for me. I pack up my laptop, or a manuscript and box of sharpened pencils, and head for the nearest McDonald's. Something about the ambient noise helps me concentrate. I also find it useful to go to the library when I'm itching for a change of scene.

Many writers find that working in nature is a great way to get the creative juices flowing. Some retreat to a cabin in the woods or near a lake. Others take their writing outside. I was recently finishing a book while speaking at a conference in Kennebunkport, Maine. I sat on a lounge chair, watching the sunset over the Atlantic as I completed the tedious but necessary task of checking my references. The gorgeous scenery turned a nasty job into a palatable one.

You might also find that holing up in a hotel for a few days is helpful. I've done this a couple of times when I really needed to concentrate and finish a project. Along these same lines, I often get a lot of writing done when I'm on the road. I think it's because I don't have the distractions I do when I'm at home. Also, especially if I'm traveling by air, I have long periods of time to wait. I've edited many a manuscript, including this one, in airports or in flight.

Institute a Writing Cloister

Another useful strategy is to institute a writing cloister: a time where you do nothing but write and sleep. Bruce Holland Rogers (2005) described how this is a useful strategy for him when he needs to get some work done but has been dawdling and wasting time at his desk: "When I'm stuck in an unproductive pattern, it can feel like I may never be productive again. The full-on practice of discipline for two days jolts me back on track" (p. 18). The cloister allows you to reprogram that time and make it productive. Rogers offered some suggestions about how this can be done:

- *Banish distractions.* He first recommended that you keep yourself away from anything that can cause you to wander off and waste time. That means no surfing the Internet, playing computer solitaire, or (for him) even reading, because all of these activities keep him from writing.
- *Have timed writing times and breaks.* Rogers has found it useful to set a timer to designate when he needs to write and when he can take a break. For example, for every hour he writes, he gives himself a 15-minute break.
- *Watch out for hazards.* There are moments in any block of writing time when you know you may have difficulties. Plan for those. Rogers described how his normal morning routine is pretty slow and laid back—he eats breakfast, checks e-mail, and has some tea. When he is cloistered, he does none of those things because they can eat up an entire morning. He prepares the night before so he can get to writing right away.

You may find the writing cloister technique helpful if you are having trouble getting started or getting past a certain point in your writing. Even if you can take only half a day, you may be astounded by how much you can get done.

Time Management by Project Type

Another time-budgeting issue has to do with the type of project you undertake. Would it be easier for you to work on one large project or several smaller ones? In the early stages of your writing career, you may not be sure what you want to write. Part of this decision comes down to what you are inspired to write, but writer Kelly James-Enger (2005) offered some additional suggestions about how to decide what type of project to undertake.

- Do you have a great idea for a book? Your deliberation process about what type of project to work on will be shorter if you do. If so, you may want to pitch your book idea to a publisher before you begin writing. It might also help you to flesh out your book idea by writing articles first. And these may help you land a book contract because an editor might be worried about whether you can write well, especially for a general audience. Your articles can help prove that you can. On the other hand, you may be able to persuade your editor with your sample chapters (see chap. 10).
- Can you work 9 months to a year on a single project? As I mentioned earlier, it can be difficult to set aside the time to work on a book. I had to write three or four books before I was no longer shocked at how much work was involved. If you are unsure about that type of time commitment, you may want to start small by writing articles.

- Do you like pitching ideas? When writing for magazines or newsletters, you spend a lot more time pitching ideas to editors. In these days of e-queries, that is less onerous than it once was. But it can still take time. In contrast, when you pitch a book idea, you only have to do that once. So much depends on your personal preference.
- What is your schedule like? If you're like most academics, you already have quite a bit on your plate. You may find it easier to work shorter pieces around your schedule than one long project.
- Which project will be most beneficial to you or your career? As noted earlier, writing books will establish you as an expert, and that can lead to speaking, consulting, and even writing articles. In contrast, articles demonstrate to a publisher that you have a platform or audience for the information you want to share. That will benefit you when you want to publish a book.

I've found that a combination of books and articles works for me. This variety keeps me moving and lets me explore a wide range of topics.

WRITING WITH CHILDREN

Some of our most challenging time-management issues can come from members of our own families. Carving time out to write when living only with adults is hard enough. But trying to write around the needs of children is even more challenging. Although writing is expected in an academic career, it is something that you often need to do in addition to your "day job." Trying to find a few extra minutes to write can seem impossible—especially if you have young children. Even so, you might find that writing is a way to save your sanity during a stressful time of life. Susan Barnson-Hayward (2005) offered a few practical suggestions to help you write while still being available to your children.

Try Getting Up Early or Staying Up Late

Generally, I don't recommend this strategy because most Americans, especially women, need to sleep more than they do. But if writing is keeping you sane or allowing you to do work you feel compelled to do, the trade-off might be worth it. Twenty to 30 minutes of focused time can be enough to get a substantial amount done.

Make Sure You Are Ready to Write

If you have limited time, you need to be ready to roll as soon as you start to write. Use the techniques I described previously. Get in the habit of keeping your materials together. Keep portfolios handy so you can grab things when you go somewhere and have a chance to work in unexpected periods of time. This will allow you to use your limited time as effectively as possible.

Child Care

If possible, try to write when you still have child care, especially for younger children. That way, you can concentrate completely. It will also allow you to make phone calls without kids hooting in the background (although I've made plenty of phone calls like that).

In summary, while your children are young, it can be especially difficult to find time to write. And you might decide you can't during this phase of your life. That's reasonable and is your choice to make. On the other hand, writing can be an oasis of sanity during a stressful time. Only you can decide if that's doable or is best deferred.

GET SOCIAL SUPPORT

My final suggestion is less a matter of time management than life management: Make sure you have people in your life who support your writing efforts. The truth is that writing can sometimes involve "paying your dues." People will probably tell you no. Even when published, you may get rotten reviews. You need people in your life who love you anyway, will tell you that you did a good job, and will not make you feel guilty about the time you take to write. Seek out these relationships and treat these people well. They will help you succeed and be there to enjoy success with you when it happens.

Conclusion

Finding time to write is a challenge for most authors. Do what you can to make it easy, and make conscious decisions about whether this is a good time in your life to write. If it's not, defer it without guilt. We often passively defer writing because we are waiting for a mythic "block of time" to suddenly appear. I hate to break it to you, but it probably never will. If you want to write, learn to take maximum advantage of smaller bits of time. And be sure to reward yourself along the way. You've done something wonderful with your time. Take a moment to celebrate.

3

Why We Bore: The Seven Deadly Sins of Academic Writers

Clutter is the disease of American writing. We are a society strangling in unnecessary words, circular constructions, pompous frills, and meaningless jargon.
—*William Zinsser (1985, p. 2)*

There's a great old joke about the optimistic versus pessimistic child. The pessimistic child was given a whole room full of toys but found problems with each and every one. The optimistic child was given an entire room full of manure. The people observing these children were surprised to enter the room and find the optimistic child digging excitedly through the manure. He said, "I know there's a pony in here somewhere."

A lot of editors feel that way about academic writing. The more optimistic editors are convinced that amid the pile of pages, there must be a pony. And so they are willing to dig. But not all editors are, especially outside of academe. Therefore, it is in your best interest to make their job easier and help them to "find the pony" in your work.

In this chapter, we're switching gears a bit and focusing on editing your work. I review some of the bad habits—or "deadly sins," if you will—of academic writers and what you can do to increase your readability. Avoiding these deadly sins will likely improve both your science writing and your less technical fare. Even if your sentences start out looking like the ones I've described below, you can edit them to make them better. Editing will take your lumpen academic prose and transform it into something sleek and beautiful. Let's get cracking!

1. Passive Voice

Passive voice is probably the most common sin of academic writing. With passive voice, you need more words to express your thoughts, and the verbs you use seldom convey action. In most cases, passive voice makes sentences long and gaseous. The result is dull, dull, dull. Below is an example of what I mean. I pulled this sentence at random from one of the books on my desk. In this case, the author used passive voice to describe the program they used.

> The curriculum was administered over the course of 11 weeks as designed. At its conclusion, a focus group was conducted to broadly assess the domains of impact as experienced by the participants.

These sentences have several examples of passive voice. Apparently, no one is doing anything. It's all being done to them. Let's see what happens when we change this to active voice.

> We administered the curriculum over 11 weeks. When the study was complete, we conducted a focus group and asked participants how the program affected their lives.

Not only is this easier to read, but you suddenly get a sense that there are real people conducting this study, and they want to know how their program changed people's lives. That's a heck of lot more interesting, and a general audience would have no trouble understanding what these researchers did.

2. JARGON

Jargon is another hallmark of academic writing. Jargon is using insider's language or specialized terms that people outside the field don't know. Before you drag out that big word, ask yourself whether your reader will understand it. Your goal as a writer is to communicate with your reader. If you are using unfamiliar terms, unless you define them you are not communicating. It is interesting that people who don't know their field well are often the ones who resort to jargon to impress their readers. Yet excessive use of jargon may make the opposite impression (Cheney, 2005).

Psychiatrist and neuroscientist Bruce Perry once told me that if he finds himself relying on jargon and technical terminology, it means he doesn't understand the concept thoroughly enough. I mention him because Perry has a real gift for communicating, both in writing and speaking. His work focuses on how trauma impacts the developing brain. This topic typically makes people's eyes glaze over. But Perry can explain it in a way that makes these complex research findings come to life. Because of this ability, he is in high demand as a consultant and speaker. He has also done a lot to encourage researchers in the child maltreatment field to integrate neuroscience research into their studies.

Below is an example of a sentence that uses three jargony terms—*self-efficacy*, *symptomatology*, and *temperament*—that are meaningful to psychologists but probably less meaningful to people outside the field. What's tricky about these words is that they can mean something different to a lay reader than they do to the person who conducted the study. If writing for a broader audience, then the authors would need to define them:

> As expected, maternal self-efficacy beliefs correlated negatively with mothers' depressive symptomatology and perceptions of infant temperament . . .

Even the term *depressive symptomatology* probably means something different to a lay reader, who may assume that it is the same as *depression*, which it may or may not be. If *depression* is an appropriate substitute, then it will be clearer and less wordy to say so.

The second half of this sentence actually does a better job of explaining their findings:

> . . . indicating that mothers felt less efficacious as parents when their depression levels were high and when they perceived their infants as difficult.

The authors could have probably cut the first part of their sentence. They also could have simplified some of the wording, substituting *effective* for *efficacious*, and *symptoms* for *symptomatology*. Here's a possible revised version.

> Mothers felt they were less effective as parents when they were depressed and their infants had difficult temperaments.

We could even rearrange the sentence to emphasize that depression and infant temperament are influenced by maternal self-efficacy:

> Mothers who were depressed and had infants with difficult temperaments considered themselves less effective as parents.

Here's another example. The first sentence uses jargon:

> Indeed, the ecological approach to the study of child maltreatment has revealed that the most powerful correlates of child neglect relate directly to economic and social factors.

The sentence that follows in the text does a better job of defining the vague terms used above:

> Child neglect is related to poverty and low income, and child maltreatment is more likely in families without access to adequate resources in the community.

The authors may be able to cut the first clause of the sentence completely. The second clause says what they need and is much clearer. It is still somewhat wordy and has weak verb constructions, but it is a definite improvement.

Jargon is not always a bad thing and is appropriate within some specialized fields (Cheney, 2005). Just this morning, I was writing an article for *Breastfeeding Abstracts*, a publication for health care providers. In it, I happily used the phrase *Lactogenesis II*, referring to the time 3 to 4 days after birth when a woman's milk becomes more plentiful. Using that concise term was elegant and saved me a couple of sentences of explanation. But it would have been a disaster in a general-audience piece. Cheney (2005) pointed out that occasional use of jargon is fine as long as we put it in a context that makes its meaning clear. He suggested that we might slip in a word or phrase that means something similar that will both make the meaning clear and educate readers about what the word means.

3. ABSTRACTIONS

Writing instructor Bruce Henderson always used to tell me to put some people in my sentences. This is great advice and will help you minimize *abstractions*. *Abstract* sentences are those with no people (or at least no peoplelike characters). Adding people to your sentences is also a great way to avoid some of the windiness of academic writing and make it more accessible and real. Here's an example of an abstract sentence:

> Elsewhere, we have suggested a more general model based on evolutionary theory to attempt to begin to conceptualize the wide range in sexual outcomes associated with a history of abuse.

This sentence refers to sexual outcomes that occur in the wake of childhood abuse. The authors were speculating on whether some of these outcomes might have adaptive significance—that is, increase the chance that the victim might develop these behaviors as a way to survive. So that's what the authors needed to say:

> In another article, we described a model based on evolutionary theory to help us understand whether outcomes we see in sexual abuse survivors might have developed to help them survive their experiences.

Here's another example of an abstract sentence. This one addresses the specific issues that practitioners face working with HIV-positive women. The authors mention one group of people—women with HIV. But they don't mention the other group—those who develop secondary trauma:

> Debriefing of secondary trauma may be helpful because of the challenging and sometimes overwhelming task of providing treatment for HIV-positive women who often have chaotic lives, disclose sexual abuse and other traumatic experiences, experience multiple illnesses, and address death.

The first part of this sentence is pretty vague. First of all, who has secondary trauma? It is most likely the therapists. So let's start there:

> Therapists working with HIV-positive women may develop secondary trauma because the needs of these clients can be overwhelming.

We needed to add some words because the information in this sentence is so abstract. We'll need to add three other sentences to describe why these clients are a challenge.

> These clients often have chaotic lives, disclose sexual abuse or other traumatic experiences, and have multiple illnesses. In addition, these women are facing death. Debriefing for therapists working with these women may be helpful.

We now have four sentences where there was only one. But the thought is much clearer, and we have a very good sense of how and why therapists might be affected by their work.

Here's another example of an abstraction:

> Most researchers have focused on the role of parenting practices as a central feature of family influences in crime.

This sentence is not horrible, but it is pretty wordy. The authors start out well with "most researchers" instead of "Research has shown," a more typical academic construction. The problem is that it's still vague. Let's make it more concrete.

> Researchers have considered parenting practices the prime family influence in crime.

This is a little better, but it is still abstract. The next question an editor would ask is what the authors mean by "parenting practices." From context, I think it is safe to assume that the authors don't mean all parenting practices. What they probably mean is "harsh" parenting, which could range from yelling to physical abuse. Harsh parenting also implies chronicity, with a single incident being less problematic than chronically harsh parenting.

"Crime" is also abstract. What do the authors mean? Who's going to commit the crime? From context, the authors probably meant the children. So it will be less abstract if they say so. The authors have implied directionality: that harsh parenting increases crime. Again, it's probably better to just say so:

> Researchers have found that harsh parenting, particularly when chronic, increases the likelihood that children will grow up to commit crimes.

Although this round of edits added to the word count, in the long run it will probably save words, because the authors have clearly stated what they are interested in. Because of that, they won't have to add extra sentences to bolster this sentence.

4. NOUN PILE-UPS

A problem that overlaps considerably with abstractions and passive voice is *noun pile-ups*. When a sentence is abstract with a passive verb construction, it uses more nouns and modifiers to get the point across. Chaos results:

> Consistent with an interactional perspective on development, there is evidence of complex interactive linkages between multiple systems.

This is a dandy. In a short 17 words, the authors managed to squeeze in five abstract nouns, with two modified by one or more adjectives. Let's start with the first clause to see whether it can be made more concrete:

> Consistent with the theory that children develop by interacting with their environment . . .

In the next half of their sentence, the authors describe the results of previous research. These studies provided evidence that a lot of factors influenced the outcome of interest and that there were links between them:

> . . . previous studies demonstrated that many factors are related to the outcome and that these factors interact with each other in complex ways.

This is better, but still pretty vague. For example, the authors might want to specify which factors make a difference and what outcomes they are studying. Let's pretend we know what those are. A revised version could read something like this:

> Poverty, community safety, and parental involvement all interact with each other and influence how children perform in school.

In this case, we have specified the factors that influence children and specified the outcome (i.e., school achievement). Even though this version has five nouns, they are concrete, making it substantially clearer and more readable.

For another example of a noun pile-up, let's take a sentence edited in one of the earlier sections of this chapter:

> Most researchers have focused on the role of parenting practices as a central feature of family influences in crime. (word count: 19)

In a short 19 words, the authors managed to squeeze in 5 nouns, 4 with modifiers. To revise this, let me ask some questions. First of all, do we need to include "researchers"? Because they are really not the central focus, could we simply state the finding and reference it? And as I mentioned earlier, it is really not "parenting practices" that increase crime, but harsh parenting. So how about this?

> Harsh parenting is the single most important influence in crime.

Or,

> Criminals have often experienced harsh punishment as children.

Or,

> Harsh punishment increases children's risk for committing crimes as they mature.

To make your work readable, keep an eye on how many nouns you use in a sentence, especially those with abstract meanings. The more you have, the higher your chances of being wordy and vague. Cut the number of nouns you use, or at least make them more concrete. And choose nouns that are precise over those that need the help of modifiers (Tapply, 2005b). Your readers will thank you.

5. WEAK VERB CONSTRUCTIONS

Part and parcel with passive voice and abstract nouns are *weak verb constructions*. Verbs are—or should be—the workhorses of a sentence. Novelist William Tapply (2005b) wrote that the more information you can convey with a verb, the better your sentence. Sometimes, we have weak verb constructions because we use nouns in their place. Turn your nouns into verbs, and watch your writing suddenly come to life. Here are some examples:

> She made a suggestion.
> He made an offer.
> That was his intention all along.

On the surface, these sentences sound fine. They have people in them. There are active verbs. And they are short. But look what happens when we change nouns into verbs:

> She suggested.
> He offered.
> He intended that all along.

It cuts the word length of the first two sentences in half and increases the readability of all three.

Sentences with weak construction often have "there" with various forms of "to be." According to Theodore Cheney (2005), in *Getting the Words Right*, "*there* itself is not bad; it's the company it keeps that gets it in trouble. *There* usually hangs out innocently on the corner with other idlers: verbs like *is, was, have been, had been*, and other weak verbs of being" (p. 34).

Here's another example:

In addition, there is overlap between these disorders.

Try this instead:

In addition, these disorders overlap.

Here's another example of a noun (*predictor*) that could be a verb:

A history of physical or sexual abuse is a powerful predictor of subsequent increased health care utilization.

Even without making drastic changes, we can improve this sentence by changing the noun to a verb:

A history of physical or sexual abuse powerfully predicts subsequent increases in health care utilization.

The sentence will be even better if we rework it further and try to get at what the author is implying. I'll first include the people this affects, and I'll also change *utilization* to *use*:

> Patients with a history of physical or sexual abuse use more health care services than people without a history of abuse.

You can simplify this even further, depending on your audience:

> Patients who were abused as children go to the doctor more often than nonabused patients.

Here's another example:

> Parents who are highly punitive sometimes are inattentive or neglectful.

Let's change these descriptors to verbs:

> Parents who harshly punish their children sometimes ignore or neglect them as well.

Once you have identified the idlers in your sentence, replace them with stronger verbs, ones that don't need to be propped up with adverbs (Tapply, 2005b). As I mentioned earlier, verbs should be the workhorses of your sentences. You can convey so much with verbs that you may not even need modifiers. For example, think about all the ways people can walk about a room: They can strut, amble, stroll, skip, gallop, limp, or run. Each of these brings up a vivid picture, and we don't need to add modifiers to get our point across. Think about ways people can sit: They can plop, ease into, sprawl, lower themselves, or drop.

In summary, paying attention to verb constructions can dramatically improve your writing. Don't worry about these as you write your first draft. But as

Cheney (2005) recommended, when it's time to edit, be on the lookout for forms of *to be* and words like *there*. These often mean that weak verb constructions are afoot. As you change these, your tone and readability will dramatically improve.

6. Too Many Words

Academics also love long, wordy sentences. "Why use one word when five would be better?" could be our rallying cry. Cheney (2005) noted that the average person writes sentences with a mean length of 25 words. Academic sentences are generally even longer. I've edited a few from my colleagues that have been six or more lines of text—in a single sentence! In contrast, professional writers average 15 words per sentence (Cheney, 2005). That should give us pause.

The classic writing guide, *Elements of Style* (Strunk & White, 1979), commanded readers to "omit needless words" (p. 23). Let that be your mantra as well. Cheney (2005) made a similar suggestion. He advised writers to first reduce the quantity of words and then try to improve the quality of the words that remain.

So how can you do that? By following the suggestions in the rest of the chapter, you'll be well on your way. But get in the habit of questioning whether each word in your sentences is pulling its weight. If not, get rid of it. Here are a few examples:

> Sexually abused males sometimes have concerns about the effect of CSA on their gender role and sexual

orientation, as well as fears of intimacy both with men and women. (word count: 29)

Let's see what we can do with this sentence. First, whom are we talking about? Sexually abused men (not males). Instead of "have concerns," which is a fairly weak verb construction, let's say "worry." What are they worried about? That being sexually abused means that they are less masculine or even gay. And instead of "have fears of intimacy," let's say "they fear intimacy" with both men and women:

Sexually abused men sometimes worry that abuse made them less masculine, or even gay, and they fear intimacy with both men and women. (word count: 23)

The second version not only has fewer words, but it is also less abstract. Suddenly, you get a very clear picture of what these men are afraid of and how sexual abuse has affected them.

Here is another example. This sentence is so wordy that it lessens the emotional impact of what the author is saying:

Women who have had experiences that clearly constitute a rape may be in need of specialized programs. (word count: 17)

"Had experiences that clearly constitute a rape." What? Let's say this with fewer words:

Women who have been raped may need specialized programs. (word count: 9)

Or how about this?

Rape victims may need specialized programs. (word count: 6)

Here, we've cut the number of words by two thirds, and the sentence is clearer and more powerful.

Trimming the number of words in your sentences will have a dramatic impact on your readability. Don't worry about extra words as you write a first draft. But as you revise, kick out the extra words and watch how your writing improves.

7. Too Many Syllables

The Emperor Franz Joseph famously told Mozart that his music had "too many notes" and that he needed to take some out. My next suggestion is similar. It gets at the heart of many of academics' writing problems. Not only do we like having lots of words, but we also want them to be as multisyllabic as possible.

I first became sensitive to the syllable problem when doing some work for the local WIC program. WIC is the U.S. government's Special Supplemental Nutrition Program for Women, Infants and Children. Because many of the women enrolled in this program have low literacy levels, WIC handouts need to be written as simply as possible. While doing this work, I learned that one way to determine reading level is to count the total number of syllables in a sentence and divide by the number of words. The higher the mean number of syllables, the higher the reading level.

In one recent project, I collaborated with the New Hampshire Bureau of Maternal and Child Health. We wrote a handout to give to all new mothers in New Hampshire on sleeping with their babies. Lots of mothers do sleep with their babies, regardless of what their doctors say. And it is generally safe. But it is quite dangerous to fall asleep with a baby on a couch or recliner. If moms are going to sleep with their babies, we wanted them to do it safely. Our original version was something like:

> It is imperative that you not sleep with your baby on a couch, sofa, day bed or recliner as this dramatically increases your baby's risk of asphyxiation.

Most middle-class mothers would get this. But we were worried about mothers who were less skilled readers. We needed to be crystal clear. In this case, clarity was potentially a matter of life or death. Here's what we came up with.

> Don't sleep with your baby on a couch, recliner or day bed. Your baby could fall, or get stuck and suffocate.

For most general-audience pieces, you won't have to write for a fourth- or sixth-grade reading level. But it's not a bad practice to keep the syllable count in mind. High syllable counts often mean that you need to simplify your language.

The most straightforward way to simplify your language is to use simpler words. *Elements of Style* (Strunk & White, 1979) advised writers to "avoid fancy words":

> Avoid the elaborate, the pretentious, the coy, and the cute. Do not be tempted by the twenty-dollar word when there is a ten-center handy, ready and able.

Anglo-Saxon is a livelier tongue than Latin, so use Anglo-Saxon words. (pp. 76–77)

Cheney (2005) also expressed a love for words of Saxon, rather than of Latin, origin. He described how as people become more educated, or want to show others they are, they are more likely to use multisyllabic "impressive" words. Cheney pointed out that English is naturally dramatic and has a higher number of action verbs than any other European-based language. "With Saxon words, the writer is not likely to be precious and affected. . . . The sophisticated like the plain word better, while the uneducated are often impressed by fancy, flowery speech" (Surmelian, quoted in Cheney, 2005, p. 163). Novelist William Tapply (2005b) made a similar point: "In most cases, the right word is the most straightforward and familiar one. Write 'thin,' not 'pellucid' or 'transpicuous'" (p. 21).

So when given a choice, choose the more readable word. Throw in a big word from time to time for variety, but keep your average syllable count down. Your writing will be the better for it.

CONCLUSION

There are some simple things that you can do to make your writing more readable. I've summarized the suggestions from this chapter in Exhibit 3.1. When you edit your manuscript, keep this checklist nearby. By targeting the problems I've highlighted, you can dramatically improve your writing.

- Have you eliminated most instances of passive voice?
- Are you using jargon or specialized terms? If so, have you defined them?
- Are there people in your sentences?
- Are you using concrete nouns?
- Have you trimmed the number of nouns per sentence?
- Have you turned nouns into verbs wherever possible?
- Have you omitted all needless words?
- Have you simplified your words and lowered the number of syllables?

Aim for lean prose, with all words in your sentences working as hard as possible. As Tapply (2005b) stated, you really can't go wrong in your writing if you write with active verbs and specific nouns. He recommended, in short, that writers share what they know but not show off. Spewing knowledge, something academics are prone to, marks writers as "long-winded bores." His pithy advice? "Don't do it" (p. 22).

4

The Art of the Story: How Narrative Nonfiction Can Add Interest to Your Writing

One of the wonderful things about a story is that it can be anything—heroic, sad, funny, triumphant, tragic, good, evil. To tell a story well, you need to help the listener identify with the main character. . . . What happened? Who made it happen? What are the results today? Where do we need to go?
—Stephen Ambrose (2002, p. xvi)

Storytelling is a powerful technique that can be used in all types of writing. Adding stories will help you connect with audiences and bring your writing to life (Morris, 2005). If you do qualitative research, you already have some experience with the power of stories. But there may be even more you can do. In this chapter, I introduce you to the techniques of telling a good story by using narrative nonfiction. Narrative nonfiction takes the techniques of fiction writers and applies them to nonfiction (Cheney, 2001). In your writing, you tell stories about real events while using techniques such as characterization, suspense, and surprise.

THE POWER OF A STORY

According to William Kilpatrick (1983), in his book *Psychological Seduction*, stories are more likely than rational arguments to compel people to right a wrong or change a situation. And history bears this out. Stories, even fictional ones, are often behind social movements. For example, in *Uncle Tom's Cabin*, Harriet Beecher Stowe (1852/1982) told the story of a fictional slave named Eliza so compellingly that Abraham Lincoln credited Stowe with ending slavery in the United States. Stowe drew on her own experience of losing a child to write about how a slave woman might feel if her children were sold away from her. Eliza ran away to keep her child from being sold.

Stories help us make sense of the world. We crave them because they are comforting and reassuring. Author Peter Rubie (2003) described how the best attorneys are not the ones that present the most legal facts but the ones who take those facts and tell us the most convincing story.

Politicians often use stories to great effect. That's why they are always talking about the apocryphal grandmother from Arkansas who said that her prescriptions cost too much. The experience of one person illustrates a broader point and can show the realities of the group he or she represents.

Mike Mangan, a psychology professor at the University of New Hampshire, said this about telling stories:

The general audience will evaluate your work with a different set of criteria than journal reviewers. That is, they want to learn something and they want a good, compelling story. Learning the ingredients of good nonfiction—that is form, structure, scene-by-scene construction, dialogue, character development, and good solid research—has made me a better storyteller. (personal communication, December 1, 2005)

People's stories in nonfiction are helpful because they illuminate sterile theories and numbers and give faces to statistics. If you can find ways to convey facts in someone's voice, those facts are always more interesting to read (Fryxell, 2005). People love stories because they hold their interest while educating them at the same time. They take us to places we may never go and introduce us to people we may never meet. People often remember the story you told more clearly than any of your brilliant points. So if you can bring in a story that illustrates your brilliant points, so much the better.

Author Max Lucado is a master storyteller. His books contain tales of the ordinary and extraordinary, and they sell millions of copies. Here's one example from his book, *Cure for the Common Life* (Lucado, 2005). In talking about how little things can make a big difference, he described the experience of World War II pilot Bohn Fawkes. Even though Fawkes's gas tank was hit by antiaircraft guns, his plane did not explode:

Technicians opened the missiles and found them void of explosive charge. They were clean and harmless and with one exception, empty. The exception contained a carefully rolled piece of paper. On it a message had been scrawled in the Czech language. Translated, the note read: "This is all we can do for you now." (p. 115)

A narrative approach also allows your heart to guide what you write. If you have compassion for the subjects of your narrative, you'll have more compelling prose, and it will also help you get closer to the truth of their experience. Emotion can bring facts to life. We tend to learn better when emotion is involved. By dramatically telling a story, we distill a version of real life and present it to readers.

Show, Don't Tell: The Art of Description

One of the things I enjoy about movies on DVD is that they often have "behind the scenes" segments, where designers, writers, and directors talk about how they worked together to tell the story via the script, sets and costumes, and camera angle. Next time you watch a movie, pay attention to how they are telling you the story. Who is narrating it? Whose point of view is represented? How do set and costume designers tell the story without using words?

As writers, we need to capture our readers' attention through their senses. Help readers experience what your protagonist is experiencing, appealing to both their eyes and ears. When telling stories, you need to have a good sense of visual detail. You want to provide enough information so readers can "see" what you are talking about but not so much that you will bore them. It's sometimes a fine line to walk. You also need a good ear for aural detail. Are you capturing how your speakers sound? How about their behavior? Don't tell your reader that a person is cruel. Instead, describe his cruel acts and let the reader come to her own conclusion. Or as Peter Rubie recommended, "Show, don't tell" (Rubie, 2003).

Scene Tension

Another aspect of storytelling is scene tension. *Scene tension* includes the event that starts your story, the goal of your protagonist, and the conflict or opposition he or she encounters on the way to achieving the goal (Bell, 2005). What does your protagonist want and why does he want it? What obstacles does he need to overcome in order to get it?

Conflict can be of three types: human against human, human against nature, and human against self. In human-against-human conflict, the people don't necessarily have to fight each other directly; they only need to have inconsistent and competing goals. Human-against-nature conflict includes tales of people against the elements or outdoors. Some examples include chronicling a climb up Mt. Everest or describing a family surviving a hurricane. Finally, conflict can include human against self. This may involve some internal conflict, such as regret or guilt that the protagonist seeks to overcome. For all types, without information about conflict, readers won't care about what happens to your protagonist and are less likely to continue reading (Bell, 2005).

Point of View

From whose viewpoint do you want to tell the story? Your decision can have a significant impact on how that story sounds to your readers. Do you want to tell the story as a first-person account? Or do you want to narrate the story from the viewpoint of a third party observing events? Both are effective, and I have often used both techniques within a single article or book. Below are descriptions of both types.

Third-Person Narration

Sometimes, the best way for you to present a story is to summarize it yourself. It might be a tale that you heard secondhand from someone else (and therefore never had a first-person account of). Or it may be a lengthy story that you can present more concisely. Below is a story from a chapter in my book, *The Handbook of Women, Stress and Trauma* (Kendall-Tackett, 2005b):

> A reporter recently called me about a heartbreaking incident that had taken place in his community. A mother of two young children had been up all night with her two-year-old, a child with special needs. The next morning, she loaded her six-month-old in the car, and left for work. In her sleep-deprived state, she forgot

to drop the baby off at day care, and left her in the car all day. Eight hours later, when she realized what she had done, she found that her baby had died.

In this tragic story, we see the potentially devastating impact of every-day stressors in the lives of young adult women. In this chapter, I describe some common stressors for women in their second, third and fourth decades. (p. 33)

At the end of the chapter, I told another story and then tied it back to the one I presented at the beginning:

The buffering influence of social support can be demonstrated by an incident that recently took place in my community. The three-year-old son of a young couple was recently diagnosed with autism. He has a mild form, and his prognosis is good. But the news has hit this young family hard. As they shared this situation with their church, family after family spontaneously stood and pledged their support. It was amazing and moving to observe, and I know this family left church that day feeling like they would not have to face this crisis alone.

Seeing this, I have to wonder: Would support have made a difference for the woman I described at the beginning of this chapter? If her company had family-friendly policies that were real, and not lip service, could she have come in late that day or taken the day off? Could a friend have helped with some of her day-to-day responsibilities? Could she have let others know that her responsibilities were overwhelming her? Of course, we'll never know. But her experience demonstrates that the stresses women experience in their 20s, 30s and 40s are real, and can be severe. We can also see that our culture still has a long way to go to support women at this stage of life. (pp. 47–48)

I also used third-person narration in a magazine article written for mothers titled, "Making Peace With Your Birth Experience" (Kendall-Tackett, 2002). I opened the article with three brief stories:

> Angela dreamed of a natural, unmedicated birth. She was managing her labor well when suddenly the cord prolapsed. Her dream birth ended in an emergency cesarean under general anesthesia. Both mother and baby survived, and Angela is grateful for that. But she feels deeply sad that she wasn't awake to see her baby's entry into the world.
>
> Sheila planned a home birth with her family all around her. Her labor was progressing well until her midwife could not detect a fetal heartbeat. Sheila was whisked to the hospital in an ambulance, and delivered a healthy baby boy. She was able to deliver vaginally, but the fear that surrounded her delivery still lingers. She keeps replaying these events over and over in her mind.
>
> Monique was in labor for 23 hours. When things weren't progressing, her labor was augmented with pitocin with no anesthesia. She was confined to her bed during her labor and in a lot of pain. When things still hadn't progressed, her doctor decided on a cesarean section. In talking about her birth later, she was so angry that no one helped with her pain, and everyone else made all the decisions for her. (p. 44)

From these stories, I launched into a summary of what we know about women's psychological reactions to birth, and I summarized several important research studies. The magazine editor suggested that I bring readers back to the stories I presented at the beginning and let them know how things turned out. This is something that writer Tom Bentley (2005) also suggested, because it gives readers the sense of having been full circle. Here is what I did:

> For Angela, recovery took a couple of years. Fortunately, she has a great relationship with her doctor and was able to talk through some of her concerns with him. Something else that was helpful was when she found another mother who had also had a cesarean section while under general anesthesia. Just having someone else who had had a similar experience made her not feel so alone.
>
> Sheila's recovery took about a year. She had a supportive midwife, and family members who were there when she was taken away by ambulance. Sheila also found that writing about her experience was healing.
>
> For Monique, recovery was actually a very long process because her birth experience brought up some issues from her past, and issues she and her husband had between them. But there were many bright spots along the way. Monique had completely stopped breastfeeding in the hospital because there had been so much to cope with all at once. But she was able to re-lactate several months later and was able to nurse her child for over a year after that. (Kendall-Tackett, 2002, p. 47)

First-Person Accounts

People can also tell a great story in their own words. I first incorporated first-person stories in a book for nurses on postpartum depression. In that book, I wanted to summarize the research, but I also wanted to include mothers' voices along with text. I had never included narrative voices before, but I knew what I wanted the final product to be. The mothers related powerful stories that made the text come alive for readers.

In the birth-experience article I described earlier (Kendall-Tackett, 2002), I also used a first-person account. This was a story that a woman sent me after reading something I had written online. It was such a great illustration that I asked for her permission to use it. I've used this story several times. It is always powerful:

> When Peter was born, the birth itself was pain free. He was small, especially his head and shoulders, and it truly didn't hurt at all. I kept insisting I wasn't really in labor up until two minutes before he was born, when the doctor told me to lay down, shut up and push! He was born at 9:30, they told us he had Down syndrome at noon, and by 4 p.m., I was hemorrhaging so badly that I came within two minutes of death. I had to have an emergency D & C with no anesthesia (talk about PAIN!!) and a big blood transfusion.
>
> That night, they told us Peter needed immediate surgery and had to go to a hospital in another city. A very traumatic day, to say the least. And then they sent me home the next day with no mention at all that I might want to talk to somebody about any of this—the Down syndrome, the near-death experience, nothing. I can still call up those memories with crystal clarity. And whenever we hear about another couple, I have

to re-process those feelings. Interestingly, most of them relate to the hemorrhaging and D & C, not to the Down syndrome "news." They're all tied up together. Maybe it's good to remind myself every so often of how precious life is.

My third birth was excruciatingly painful—baby was 9 lbs 3 ounces, with severe shoulder dystocia—his head was delivered 20 minutes before his shoulders. I had some Stadol in the IV line right before transition, but that's all the pain relief I had. I thought I was going to die, and lost all perspective on the fact that I was having a baby. I just tried to live through each contraction. Of course, I was flat on my back, with my feet up in stirrups, and watching the fetal monitor as I charted each contraction—I think those things should be outlawed! I know now that if I had been squatting, or on my hands and knees, I probably could have gotten him out much easier. I'm the one who has the giant shoulders and incredibly long arms, so I can't blame anyone else on my two babies with broad shoulders.

That night, after Alex was born (at 9 in the morning), I could not sleep at all because every time I tried to go to sleep, my brain would start re-running the tape of labor, and I would feel the pain and the fright and the fears of dying all over again. I stayed up all that night and the next day, and didn't sleep until I was home in my own bed. (Kendall-Tackett, 2002, pp. 45–46)

Although using the narrative voice can add power and interest to your words, use stories sparingly. By themselves, stories can overwhelm what you are trying to say. Instead, weave these narrative voices throughout your text so that they highlight your points. Pay attention to whether the story continues to hold your interest, and edit accordingly.

Pacing and Rhythm of Your Story

Another factor to consider is the pacing and rhythm of your story. This has to do with subjective qualities of your story: how it sounds and flows. Although we read with our eyes, reading is largely an auditory experience.

Try reading what you have written out loud to see how it sounds. Is it compelling? If you are not sure, try reading it to someone else. (You may need to buy them lunch.) Are there parts where their eyes glaze over? Typical academic prose sounds horrible when read aloud. If you spot an academic sentence as you read, take a minute to rework it. Reading it aloud to someone else also helps you take advantage of the visual cues we get when we speak that are absent with our written words. (Nodding off is definitely not a good sign!) There are no hard-and-fast rules for this, so feel free to experiment and see what works.

There are other ways to add variety to the pace and rhythm of your writing (Rubie, 2003). I've listed them below.

Vary Sentence and Word Length

One way to move a story along is to vary the sentence and word length. Although it's generally better to have shorter sentences, throwing in a long one now and then can help the story move forward and provide interest. Similarly, short words are usually better than long ones. But throwing in an occasional long word can make for good reading.

Write Like You Speak: The Cadence of Human Speech

Another way to add interest to your writing is to write like you speak. Using the natural cadence and rhythm of human speech will hold your readers' interest and keep the story moving forward. *USA Today* columnist Craig Wilson said, "The biggest compliment you can get is that your writing sounds just like you" (quoted in Bete, 2005, p. 35).

To train your ear, start paying attention to conversations around you. What do they sound like? Although you don't need to imitate all aspects of live speech, you might notice that the verb constructions tend to be active. In addition, people use contractions; put prepositions at the end of sentences; split infinitives; start sentences, and even paragraphs, with "but"; and do all the naughty things your fifth-grade teacher said would send you straight to hell. That's because language is a living thing. Word usage changes, as does what is considered "proper" English. And whether we are aware of it or not, we get a lot of feedback when we speak. We can usually tell if we are boring people and will make adjustments in our constructions, expressions, tone, and vocabulary on the basis of these subtle (and sometimes not-so-subtle) cues. With writing, there are no such cues. And so we feel free to blab on and on, blithely unaware that our readers have just lost consciousness.

Alternate Between Narrative and Summary

Another way to add interest is by alternating between narrative and summary (Cheney, 2001). In one part of the story, you may have a first-person account. Then in the next part, you may draw back and summarize what is going on. Or you might also try alternating between facts, action, third-person narration, and direct quotations (Fryxell, 2005). Even if you can't put the information in a person's voice, narration can keep this information from seeming dry.

Catherine Koverola and Subadra Panchanadeswaran (2004) alternated between narration and summary to great effect in a chapter they wrote for a book I edited, *Health Consequences of Abuse in the Family* (Kendall-Tackett, 2004). Their chapter was on barriers to care for women of color who were experiencing family violence. They started by telling the story of Maria.

> At age 16, I came to the U.S. from Mexico. My parents had heard of a better life in the U.S., and they gave their life savings to the Coyote to bring me here. On the journey, I was raped repeatedly every night, as were most of the young girls. I became pregnant. Jose took me as his wife, and for three years he beat me daily. One

day he left me, penniless and with two small children. I spoke little English, and had few friends. But determined to survive, I looked for work in the factories of Los Angeles. A nearby mission took care of my children while I worked. (p. 49)

After telling the story of Maria, Koverola and Panchanadeswaran drew back and summarized the scene from the health care provider's perspective. They described what happened after Maria came to the hospital with multiple injuries caused by her abusive husband:

Maria's road to healing began with the intervention of a Spanish-speaking medical practitioner who used the JCAHO-recommended (Joint Commission for the Accreditation of Healthcare Organizations) screening questions. . . . Countless women who seek medical care, both acute and routine healthcare, are never screened for domestic violence, even when they present with classic domestic violence injury patterns. . . . This particular health care practitioner followed the recommended protocol of screening in private in the native language of the patient. (pp. 49–50)

After elaborating on this point further, the authors switched back to Maria's first-person narrative voice.

The nurse asked where my children were, and I told her they were at home with the neighbor. She asked if I had any friends or family who could support me. She then asked if I wanted to speak to an "advocate." She explained it was someone who could help me take the steps for safety. My journey to safety began that night. (p. 50)

By the time this chapter is finished, the authors have told us the stories of Maria, Tanya, and Min. The final result relayed a lot of information in a readable and moving way.

TIMELINE

When telling a story, you must also establish a timeline of events. What time period are you speaking about? Do all of the events on which you report take place in a day, week, month, or longer? Where your story begins and ends are the "bookends" of the story (Rubie, 2003).

You don't necessarily have to follow events chronologically. In fact, in many cases it is boring to begin at the beginning. Theodore Cheney (2001) described a technique known as *in medias res*, or the "middle of the story," which Peggy Noonan (2001) used effectively in her biography of Ronald Reagan. Rather than starting at the beginning of Reagan's life, she brought us in by describing a recent event: Former staffers and friends are gathered for the christening of the U.S.S. Ronald Reagan. The scene is compelling. Twelve years have passed since these people have seen each other. Many had had very public feuds. Some became enemies before, during, and after their time in the White House. But now, people have mellowed. Many have retired and have pursued new interests. Her description of this gathering pulls us immediately into the story:

> It was like the last gathering of the clans, the reunion of five hundred friends, cabinet secretaries, aides, staffers,

clique, tong and cabal members and appointees of Ronald Wilson Reagan, fortieth president of the United States, in Williamsburg, Virginia, on March 3, 2001. It was the biggest coming together of the Reagan hands since the day he left office, in January of 1989.

The big room in the Kingsmill Resort rocked with greeting. "I don't believe it," "Great to seeee you." . . . People with young eyes, lifted eyes, crinkled eyes from being in the sun; people with strollers, with walkers. (p. 1)

Noonan manipulated the timeline effectively for her narration, and by doing so, made us interested in knowing what happened next. You can also do this by starting at the end of the story and backtracking to how the protagonist ended up in that situation. (Think dead guy in the pool at the beginning of *Sunset Boulevard*.) My one caution is that you don't lose readers by flipping back and forth between past and present too quickly. Give your readers plenty of markers so that they know where they are.

Make Us Care

My final suggestion for good storytelling is to make people care about the problem or issue that you are writing about. Or to put it another way, you need to satisfy the "so-what" factor. Readers today can choose from so much material that if something is not interesting right from the start, they will move on to something that is. Period. According to Cheney (2001), you have 250 words (about one manuscript page) to capture a reader's attention. Indeed, your words are unlikely to see the light of day unless you can make an editor care. So if you want to get into print, the so-what factor needs to be uppermost in your mind.

Write a Compelling Beginning

The purpose of the opening paragraph is to hook the readers and then hold their interest by telling about the problem or situation facing your subject. How did your subject get to this place? What does he or she need to do next? Authors Bodie and Brock Thoene (Thoene & Thoene, 1990), in their book *Writer to Writer*, offered some suggestions for writing a compelling opening paragraph:

- *Open with a question.* Start your article or book by presenting an intriguing question. Even the most technical aspects of science can be expressed in relatively simple terms. What are you trying to say? Let's say you wanted to write something about how trauma creates physical changes in the bodies of trauma survivors. You could say: "Do traumatic events change the body? That question has intrigued scientists over the past decade. And the answer appears to be 'yes.'"

- *Use a story.* You can also start with a story. Let's say that you are writing a piece on domestic violence. Instead of statistics, tell us the story of one victim:

  Every day, Josie's life is filled with fear. She never knows what will set her husband off and cause him to beat her. It could be anything: a spilled glass of milk, a late meal, or the kids misbehaving. She describes her life as "walking on eggshells."

- *Compare and contrast.* Another technique that tends to draw people in is when you compare and contrast two competing theories or worldviews. You might, for example, compare and contrast the stories of two women's lives in a small community: one rich, the other poor. What are their hopes and dreams? What is their family life like? What do they want out of life?

  Amanda and Josephine both turned 70 this year. They have both lived in the same Southern town all of their lives. They married local boys and raised families. But there is a fundamental difference between them. Amanda is rich and Josephine is poor, and this colors their views of everything.

- *Declarative statement.* The final technique is the declarative statement. This technique practically forces you to read the next sentence. I once wrote an article on the importance of alternative work schedules for people with disabilities. After trying several different openers, I landed on this: "Work is important." It compelled people to read the next sentence, which would tell them why. From there, I built on my central thesis: the importance of flexible scheduling options for people with disabilities.

Surgeon Atul Gawande (2002) used a combination of story and declarative statement to open his book about the practice of medicine, *Complications*. He started with a story of someone who came into the emergency department with a gunshot wound to the buttocks. From this patient's symptoms, the surgeons thought the bullet had damaged the patient's bladder and colon and perhaps other internal organs. But when they opened him up, they found nothing amiss. They could not explain his symptoms, and he ended up leaving the hospital a few days later, in apparent good health. Gawande then explained,

> Medicine is, I have found, a strange and in many ways disturbing business. ... We drug people, put needles and tubes in them, manipulate their chemistry, biology, and physics, lay them unconscious and open their bodies up to the world. ... out of an abiding confidence in our know-how as a profession. What you find when you get in close, however—close enough to see the furrowed brows, the doubts and missteps, the failures as well as the successes—is how messy, uncertain, and also surprising medicine turns out to be. (p. 4)

I don't know about you, but he had my attention.

After you get past the first paragraph, you can continue to make people care by writing in an active voice, putting people in the sentence, and by telling stories—the techniques we've been discussing all along.

If there is something that your readers can do, tell them that too. It's not very satisfying to learn about a situation, especially a horrific one, without having the ability to do anything about it. Sometimes, realistically, there is little readers can do. But maybe they can write a letter. Is there a Web site where they can go for more information? What should they do if they know someone in that position? Are there agencies that can help? What can they do if the issue affects them?

Make It Real

Another way to increase the readability of your writing is to bring it down to the level of everyday life. Find a way to make it real for your readers. Don't just quote statistics; put some faces on those numbers.

In 2005, I was making a presentation to a group of nurses and lactation consultants on how breastfeeding improved infant survival worldwide. One of the studies I presented was a recent article from the journal *The Lancet*. In that article, the authors (Jones et al., 2003) described how lack of breastfeeding is responsible for approximately 1.3 million infant deaths each year. The World Health Organization has published similar figures.

When you work in any profession, after a while you become immune to the numbers. You can hear "1.3 million infant deaths," but the full horror of that number doesn't hit you. It's almost too big to even imagine. In this presentation, I wanted to get this information across in a way that would resonate with the audience.

It just so happens that I made this presentation 4 months after the 2004 tsunami struck Asia and killed more than 200,000 people. Everyone had seen pictures of unprecedented death and destruction caused by that storm. Those images were still fresh in people's minds. So after talking briefly about the tsunami and reminding people about how many lives were lost, I pointed out that the number of infant deaths due to not breastfeeding was equivalent to five or more tsunamis—every year. There were audible gasps from the audience, and I knew that I had succeeded in making that statistic real.

Conclusion

People have a natural affinity for stories. Incorporating them into your writing will make what you say more interesting and easier to remember. Start paying attention to the natural cadence and rhythm of human speech and incorporate it into your writing. Find a way to say what you want to say in someone's voice. Don't be afraid to show some emotion, and make us care about your subject. I think you'll be pleased with the results.

5

Working With Other Writers and Writers' Groups

Writers tend to be so paranoid about talking about their work because no one, including us, really understands how it works. But it can help a great deal if you have someone you have learned to trust, someone who is honest and generous and who won't jinx you. . . . On a bad day you also don't need a lot of advice. You just need to feel once again that other people have confidence in you. The members of your writing group can often offer just that.
—Anne Lamott (1994, p. 157)

Writing is generally solitary work, but it's not work you always have to do alone. There are various points in the process at which you may want to involve others. Depending on their role, others' level of involvement can vary considerably. If you are a member of a writers' group, you may only solicit occasional feedback on particular aspects or passages of your work. On the other hand, if you are working with a coauthor, your collaboration could be intense and could extend over many weeks or months. In this chapter, I briefly discuss joining a writers' group, working with a mentor, and working with a coauthor.

WRITERS' GROUPS

Opinion is decidedly mixed when it comes to the value of writers' groups. Some people swear by them. Others run away as fast as they can. I fall into the second group. That being said, you may find that a writers' group would be useful for you.

Writers are a solitary bunch, and it's often hard for people who don't write to really understand. Hanging out with other writers can be a nice source of fellowship. But go into these groups wisely. If you are considering a group, think about what you want to accomplish by being involved with it. You should also consider whether the characteristics of the group are compatible with your goals. With a few considerations, writers' groups can work for you.

In the past, I've been invited to join two local writers' groups. In both cases, I declined. The first was a community group. The writing genres were all over the place. The participants were writing poetry, short stories, and novels. Few (if any) members were writing nonfiction. None were doing anything even remotely similar to what I was doing. And that, for me, was the main reason not to join.

The second group was more informal. It consisted of a few people who were writing magazine articles for various lay publications. This was more similar to what

I was doing, but the authors were not professionals trying to communicate what they knew about their subject to a lay audience. The articles they wanted to write were personal stories or experiences. Again, it was not very similar to what I was trying to do.

For me, the clincher was what participating in these groups would entail. In each group, we would have to read each other's work and critique it weekly. Like many of you, my schedule is pretty full, and I could not justify the amount of time it would take for me to read so much work by others that was so different from my own. If a friend wants me to read something he or she has written, I usually will. But I don't feel obligated to perform this task for strangers. If you love that sort of thing, go for it. Just be careful that the group isn't taking you away from getting your own work done.

Writing, especially in the early days, is a fragile thing. You want to be able to show it to people who are going to be supportive and helpful. This is true whether you show your work to one person or many. Unfortunately, some writers' groups attract people who have never gotten their work published but nevertheless feel free to offer scathing comments to everyone else. This you do not need!

That's not to say that you don't, occasionally, need to hear something critical about your writing. If you're completely off track, it's much better to hear about it in the early stages. Some negative feedback might be necessary, but be careful whom you ask. You could be getting advice that is uninformed and, worse, that could completely stop you in your creative process. I'm very picky about the people I show my formative work to. And I'm not alone in this. Novelist Harlan Coben said, "I find criticism paralyzes me. . . . So I don't need it. The only person who reads my early drafts is my wife, and her job is to tell me that it's brilliant beyond words" (quoted in Clausen, 2001, p. 95).

Clausen (2001) dealt with one critical member of his writing group by ignoring her comments and focusing "on the obviously more intelligent members of the group who had the good sense to praise my writing lavishly" (p. 163). Joking aside, some writers describe pretty horrible experiences in writers' groups. Lamott (1994) described how some members of writers' groups feel "morally and aesthetically compelled to rip your story to shreds" (p. 153). These experiences may help you improve your writing. But honestly, I don't want this much drama in my life. In order to be your most creative, you need to be unafraid of making mistakes— even big ones. If you're worried about getting torn apart by a group, you're likely to be more cautious and less creative. So if the group you're thinking about joining has an overall negative tone, I'd advise you to steer clear of it.

Conversely, sometimes you do need some corrective feedback, and members of your group may be afraid to give it to you. Or they may be unfamiliar with the audience you are trying to reach or publication you are writing for and so are unable to offer feedback that's really helpful. And you may get an inflated view of the quality of your work. To my mind, this is less of a problem than an overly critical group. But it can still be a limitation, and you need to keep it in mind.

WRITING MENTORS

A *writing mentor* is someone who works one-on-one with you for a certain period of time. My writing mentors have been quite helpful. I would recommend this approach if you would like to give it a try. Some organizations, such as Writer's Digest and the Christian Writers' Guild, have formal mentoring programs. Or you may make a more informal arrangement. It doesn't hurt to ask someone for help. Be sure to offer to do something in kind for them. You may even be able to find a mentor through your professional association.

Mentoring relationships can also keep you accountable for meeting deadlines. Just like our students, we often underestimate how much work it will take to complete a project. You may be scrambling at the end of a project to meet your deadline. If you work on your project with a mentor, you may be able to avoid (or at least lessen) this problem.

There are a lot of ways that mentors and mentees can find each other. In my case, they were instructors in the writing courses I took while working at Stanford. The one-on-one time with the instructors, specifically going over my work, was even more valuable than what I was learning in their classes. I also had a mentor when I was an undergraduate. Calvin Sowder was one of my favorite professors (the one who really made me love my field). I worked for him, and he reciprocated by reviewing stuff I was working on.

The main thing a mentor provides that differentiates this type of relationship from what you might receive in a writers' group is the individual attention. As for which one would work best for you, that is really an issue of personal preference. Are you more comfortable in groups or in one-on-one relationships? You may also find that at different stages of your career a group (or mentor) better meets your needs. And you will likely enter into several of these types of relationships over the course of your career.

COAUTHORS AND COLLABORATORS

Some of the best work I've ever done has come from collaborating with others. In a good collaborative relationship, each person brings specific strengths to the project. And working together can lead to this incredible synergism—where what you produce together is so much better than what either of you could produce on your own.

There is also the practical aspect of sharing the work. Working with others can literally cut your work in half. And in terms of productivity, that's a very good thing.

As great as collaboration can be, please be wise in your choice of collaborators. I've had both good and bad experiences with collaborators, and I've avoided a couple of situations that I knew would have been really bad. I've also had the chance to observe some bad collaborative relationships from afar. Before "jumping into bed" with a coauthor or coeditor, consider the following.

Compatibility of Working Styles

There are a number of things you must consider before entering into an agreement with a coauthor. Being friends with someone is not enough. In fact, if a co-authorship is handled badly, it can destroy your friendship. One thing to consider when contemplating a coauthorship is the compatibility of your working styles. If you are someone who consistently meets your deadlines, you will be less than thrilled with someone who always works at the last minute. You may be fast but a little sloppy, whereas your coauthor is slow and deliberate. You may be unhappy with her pace, and she may be unhappy with your sloppiness. Differences in working style can be a plus when your collaborator makes up for areas where you are weak and vice versa. But it's better if you are aware of these differences going in, or have a frank discussion once they crop up.

Other issues can interfere. For example, I know that I couldn't work with someone who insisted on composing or working through sections over the phone. I'm a visual–kinesthetic learner, and trying to write over the phone drives me nuts (think: finger-nails-on-a-chalkboard kind of crazy). I need to see the words and have them in my hands. I also become very impatient with someone who tinkers with every word and is endlessly revising.

Even when your work styles are different, however, you may be able to work together well. It's important to be realistic about what you want out of the relationship and to recognize and acknowledge differences in style right from the beginning. Differences can actually increase the value of your collaboration. So they can be worth working through.

Quality of Work and Contribution

Something else to consider is the quality of your collaborator's work. Over the years, I've worked with several different folks on various projects where I knew I would be doing most of the writing. Many of these colleagues were clinicians or had some other type of hands-on experience that made them valuable contributors to the project. But they weren't writers. I usually knew this going in and was willing to accommodate them. And there may be situations like this for you as well, where the quality of contributions of your coauthor or coeditor may outstrip a strict 50/50 division of labor.

Another factor to consider is timeliness of work. There are real deadlines in the publishing world. Will your collaborator be able to meet them? Or is he or she someone who is always weeks or months behind? Academics are notoriously bad at meeting deadlines. Even nonacademics can have terrible organizational skills and never manage to get work done in a timely manner.

That being said, there may be times when a collaborator has such an important contribution to make that it's worth the extra headaches of missed deadlines. If your potential collaborator is this way, you will need to have an open discussion at the beginning in which you simply state that you know that this is a problem and that this is how you plan to address it. The more structure you can provide for your coauthor, the better. And give them a generous deadline (well ahead of when you actually need the material) so that you won't get horribly behind if they miss their deadline. You might even offer to draft some of their materials to help them get started.

CONCLUSION

Collaborating with others can increase the richness of your writing and reduce your workload, and it may add valuable substance to your work. But be cautious before jumping into an arrangement until you've considered whether your partner is compatible with your working style. And it's better if you can be up front with what you see as potential problems and what you can do to address them.

6

Preparing Your Final Manuscript for Submission

Believe it or not, keeping moving in writing is even more important than getting started. . . . Some of the most highly published authors in the world, whose books and articles we see everywhere, are not necessarily artists of the English or any other language. They are good, workmenlike writers who are organized and determined.
—Don Aslett and Carol Cartaino (2001, p. 209)

In chapters 1 through 5, we discussed strategies for improving your basic product—your writing! However, in your anxiety to get your perfect prose out to your editor, it's important not to overlook the practical details of submitting your product. That's the subject of this chapter. You'll need to check that your manuscript is carefully put together and that all the components are present and in order. You'll need to format your manuscript according to your publisher's guidelines. And last but not least, you'll need to make sure that you include the required paperwork, such as permission to cite the work of others. Delivering a well-prepared, complete package will make your editor happy and will help to ensure that the production process goes more quickly and smoothly. Many of the suggestions I mention here will be more applicable to books than to articles. But some, like making sure your writing has international appeal or complying with fair-use guidelines will apply to either.

SEEING YOUR MANUSCRIPT AS A WHOLE

A book or a longer manuscript is something you often craft piece by piece. But eventually, all these pieces need to work together. To facilitate this process, I'd like to pass along a suggestion I learned from Dan Poynter's (2003) book, *Writing Non-Fiction*. Poynter has written more than 60 books, so I tend to trust his advice. He suggested that you start thinking of your book as a whole right from the start by putting it all together in a binder or notebook. He suggested going even further than that. Make a cover for yourself. Even write some back material with a paragraph-long description of your book.

This may sound hokey, but it works fabulously well. I first tried it with a book I was editing. Once all my chapters were in a notebook, I could suddenly see where chapters overlapped with each other and proceeded to cut repetitious passages. It also helped me begin to make interconnections between the chapters, something I couldn't do when I was handling chapters as individual manuscripts. I've used this technique on every book since then (including this one). And it continues to work for me.

REFERENCE STYLE

Something you want to find out early in the writing process is your publisher's preferred reference style. Your publisher may have a style sheet that they can send to you or that you can grab off of their Web site. They may also include a copy with your contract. Use this. It will tell you how to cite your references in the text and at the end of the article or book. Starting in one style and having to convert your references to another is a pain and can lead to lots of typos. Although typos are not the end of the world, they do make you look less professional.

As for overall style, the two style manuals I've used most often are *The Chicago Manual of Style* (University of Chicago Press, 2003) and the *Publication Manual of the American Psychological Association* (American Psychological Association [APA], 2001). If you plan to do a lot of writing, then it's probably good to have both. I use APA style most of the time, and it feels like my first language when it comes to references. However, I've found that a lot of magazine editors and some trade publishers prefer Chicago style.

Before you submit your final draft, be sure to cross-check all your references. Make sure that everything you've cited in your text is listed identically in the reference list, and everything listed in the back is cited in the text. This can be a tedious task, but it will save you time later on.

HEADERS

Headers can dramatically increase the readability and marketability of your book. Think about a potential customer, flipping through your book, trying to decide whether they want to buy it. Back material and reviews will influence them, but so will your headers. Buyers can tell a lot about what's in your book by your headers and subheaders. Be sure and take full advantage of this by using enough of them in your text. If you don't, your editors may insert more. And their headers may not be the best way to describe your content. On the other hand, you don't want to have so many headers that the final product looks too busy. So use some discretion, and try to picture what the printed work will look like.

Headers can be at various levels. Publishers refer to them as *A-level* when they designate an entire major section. Then you have *B-level*, all the way down to *E-level*. When it comes time to turn in your manuscript, format your headers using your publisher's style. Some publishers use location of the header to indicate major versus minor headers. So for this type of style, major headers are in the middle of the page. Secondary headers are at the left margin, then indented, then at the start of a paragraph. Other publishers prefer that all headers be at the left margin, with major versus minor determined by font size and style (e.g., italicized, boldface).

WRITING FOR ENGLISH-SPEAKING AUDIENCES OUTSIDE THE UNITED STATES

As publishing becomes more international, it behooves you to become aware of English-speaking audiences outside of the United States. Readers in Canada, the United Kingdom, Ireland, Australia, and New Zealand are used to different spellings of words, such as *behaviour* versus *behavior*, *colour* versus *color*, and *surprize* versus *surprise*. Be aware that countries outside of the United States use metric measurements for temperature, length, volume, and weight. I don't know about you, but I don't think in metric. Someone could tell me that it was 30 °C outside, and it would mean next to nothing to me. Readers from other countries often have a similar reaction when reading nonmetric measurements. A simple solution is to use both if you think your writing may be read in another country. I did this in a recent book because I knew we would have readers in Canada, the United Kingdom, Australia, and New Zealand. When we referenced measured units like ounces or inches, we made sure to include their metric equivalents.

Colleagues and friends sometimes share with me their observations of additional differences between English in the United States and in other English-speaking countries. I mention a few here to raise your awareness that such differences do exist. Rosemary Gordon of New Zealand (NZ), for example, noted that

> each country has its own colloquialisms of course, but I suspect that people in NZ are more familiar with American ones than Americans are of NZ ones, purely because of the influence of the media, especially TV, films, and music. Plus, NZ has made quite a few Maori words mainstream, which are largely unfamiliar outside NZ: *whanau, iwi, aroha*, and so on. You know there's a whole unit on NZ English in the Year 13 English curriculum; far too much to fit into a paragraph! Then there are the spelling differences. Americans leave letters out! *Programme, colour, paediatrics, counsellor.* I could go on forever! (personal communication, January 4, 2006)

Rachel O'Leary of Great Britain offered another insight: "When you say 'the holidays' in the USA, you mean the Christmas/Hanukah/New Year period. When we say 'the holidays,' we mean the July–August school holidays" (personal communication, January 5, 2006).

CITING OTHER PEOPLE'S WORK: PERMISSIONS AND FAIR USE

No discussion of preparing your manuscript is complete without a mention of permissions needed to quote someone else's work. U.S. copyright law ensures that authors' expressions are protected. (For more on this, see chap. 11.) That means if you are using an author's exact phrasing or sequence of words to express an idea, then you need permission to cite more than what can be considered "fair use." According to the fair-use rule, authors may make limited use of others' material without permission. But the guidelines for what constitutes fair use are much more vague than you might suspect (Fishman, 2004a). Indeed, fair use is considered an "affirmative defense," meaning that the burden of proof is on you to demonstrate that your use of the author's materials falls within these guidelines. There are four guidelines to help you determine whether something falls under fair use. These are listed below. Intellectual property attorney Stephen Fishman (2004a) suggested "if in doubt, seek legal advice or get permission" (p. 11/4).

The first fair-use guideline is the purpose and character of the use. The key question is whether your use is somehow *transformative*—that is, adds to or extends the existing knowledge base. This can often be a key factor that overrides other considerations. If your use of the material merely substitutes for the original, then it is less likely to be considered fair use. Some examples of fair use include when your use is for comment, criticism, or parody of an existing work, or if your use is part of news reporting or is for research or scholarship (Fishman, 2004a; Wilson, 2003; Zaharoff, 2005).

The second fair-use guideline is the nature of the prior work. Someone's unpublished work has much more protection than published work. Using someone's unpublished materials without permission and simply citing them is not fair use. Authors should always have the opportunity to be first to publish their materials

(Zaharoff, 2005). If your publication would deny them that opportunity, then your use of that material infringes on their copyright (Fishman, 2004a; Wilson, 2003).

The third fair-use guideline has to do with the amount and substantiality of the material used. It is always up to the user to consult the copyright holder (often, but not always the publisher of the work) to find out what they consider to be fair use. If what you've cited is a large proportion of a short work (e.g., song lyrics, poetry), then even if the total number of words is small, it is not fair use. Even in longer works, if the part you've chosen to quote is the critical heart of the work, then that may not be fair use (Zaharoff, 2005). Fishman (2004a) suggested that authors quote no more than a "few successive paragraphs from a book or article, one or two lines from a poem, or take no more than one graphic, such as a chart, diagram or illustration" (p. 11/10). However, note again that publishers and copyright holders have their own standards for fair use that may be less than—or may exceed— the examples given above. The information is often available on publishers' Web sites.

The final fair-use guideline is whether your quotation from the work would have an impact on its market value (Wilson, 2003; Zaharoff, 2005). This includes not only the economic impact of your use of the material but the impact if others were to follow suit and do the same thing (Fishman, 2004a). Copier giant Kinko's lost a copyright infringement lawsuit. They were copying articles from other sources, compiling them into anthologies, and selling them to students. In this case, their actions cut into the profits of the legitimate copyright owners, and they had to pay more than half a million dollars in fines as a result (Wilson, 2003). Copyright may also apply to any derivative work that is so similar to the original that it could impact the sale of the original (e.g., your writing of a play with a plot highly similar to that of a recently published novel).

I strongly advise you to secure reprint permissions as soon as you realize you may need them. The process of querying for permission and waiting for the required paperwork to be sent from busy permissions offices can take several months. Some publishers won't charge you for permissions, whereas others will charge a nominal fee. For example, I recently had to pay $75 each for permission to reprint the diagnostic criteria for major depressive disorder and posttraumatic stress disorder from the *Diagnostic and Statistical Manual of Mental Disorders* (4th ed., text revision; American Psychiatric Association, 2000), even though I had paraphrased the material.

SUBMITTING YOUR WORK

Before finally submitting your work, take a moment to carefully proofread it one more time. You might also ask someone else to proofread your manuscript. I've had to face the fact that I'm a lousy proofreader of my own material. The types of mistakes I make are leaving out small words in sentences. I miss these in my own writing because my mind fills in what is supposed to be there. Typos are embarrassing, so do your best to find them before you send in the manuscript. But don't get so hung up on finding every last one that you miss your deadline.

So your work has been proofread and everything is ready to go. The final thing you need to know before you send your "baby" off is the format for submitting it. More and more publishers are asking for things to be submitted electronically. If that is the case, ask whether they would like your manuscript as one long file or broken down by chapters. Also, find out their preference for pagination. Some publishers want consecutive pagination. This is understandable but in my view a royal pain. If they want consecutive pagination, go into each chapter and manually enter the page number where you want the chapter to start. Don't make these changes in pagination until the absolutely final draft, because any changes you make may change things by a page—throwing off all the work you've just done. When doing this, take your time so that you don't make a mistake. Be sure to also include all of the front matter (acknowledgments, table of contents, dedication [if any], and title pages), photographs, and tables and figures. If your publisher prefers to receive a hard copy, print out all of the pages and assemble them into a manuscript pile. I've found that it takes an hour to an hour and a half to print and assemble hard copies of everything I need to send when sending an average 250-page manuscript, so be sure to allow time for this so you will not be rushed and make mistakes. I burn a CD with all of the electronic files on it. And I include any written permissions I need to send, always keeping copies for my files. When I have assembled the entire package, I usually send it via FedEx or UPS so I know that it will arrive safely.

Most publishers will give you a manuscript check-list so you can make sure you include everything. Keep track of that list. I usually file it with my contract, because it tends to come with it. That way, when it's time to grab it, I know right where it is.

START A REVISION FILE

This last suggestion may sound strange—thinking about revisions before your manuscript even appears in print. But I can almost guarantee you that as soon as your manuscript is beyond your grasp, an important study will come out on your topic. Don't despair! Add it to your revision file.

A revision file is where you put any new research that has come out on a topic since you turned in your last set of edits. It's also where you can put any notes about typos you find in your text or other changes you would like to make. I have a revision file for each of my books. My revision files are also helpful when I make presentations or write articles based on my books. They give me one place to keep any new research so

I'll know just where to look and can incorporate it easily. And when it's time to write a revised version of the book, I already have a major head start. I recommend that you start a file too.

Conclusion

Getting your work ready to submit can take more time than you might expect. Be sure to allow ample time to complete this final phase. After you deliver your manuscript to your publisher, go out for a nice dinner to celebrate. You've done something huge and important. At the very least, you deserve a lovely meal.

7

The "E" Word:
Working Well With Editors

Don't expect the editor to proclaim your work a pleasure
to read and . . . [that] your talent is clearly exceptional.
If you want love and acceptance, get a dog.
—*Elaura Niles (2005, p. 139)*

Whenever it's award time in the entertainment industry, stars always tell interviewers that it's "an honor to be nominated." And to be sure, it really is. We expect the stars to say that, seeing as it's the gracious, humble thing to say. But let's face it; what they are really thinking is that it's much better to win!

Authors are the same way. We'll bravely say that we gain a great deal from feedback (and "it's an honor to be nominated"), and that may be true. But what we'd really like for our editors to tell us is that every phrase that drips from our fingers is a pearl and that we don't need to change a word. That may happen—for a few of you. For the rest of us mortals, editors are here to help. And they will do that by going over what you've written with a fine-tooth comb.

Authors often have mixed feelings about their editors. Take a look at almost any book, and the author is thanking his or her editor. Of course, I really wouldn't expect them to say, "My editor was a crazed egomaniac who made my life a living hell." That wouldn't be particularly smart, even if true. And then there was this funny note at the beginning of *The Devil Wears Prada*. Author Lauren Weisberger (2003) thanked four key people, one of whom was her editor: "Stacy Creamer—my editor. If you don't enjoy the book, blame her . . . she edited out all the really funny stuff" (unnumbered page). But usually, authors express sincere thanks, showing that authors and editors can work together for the greater good.

Editors are our safety nets. They are the ones who help us to be clear and who keep us from saying stupid things in print. For example, in one of my first general-audience publications, the editor quietly edited out all my smart-assed asides (e.g., "pul-LEEZE"). I'm so glad she did. It would have been quite embarrassing if those had been published. But they seemed inspired at the time I wrote them.

So suck it up, and realize that editing is part of the process. And because of its critical nature, you may not always enjoy it. In fact, the first couple of times, it may feel like having your limbs amputated. (And speaking for myself, I've never gotten entirely used to it.) But it's for your own good. And I promise to help you through it.

Making the Most of
Editorial Relationships

I normally have a great working relationship with my editors. One recent experience was with Carole Honeychurch at New Harbinger Publications when she edited *Breastfeeding Made Simple* (Mohrbacher & Kendall-Tackett, 2005). I had worked with Honeychurch before and always found her comments helpful. What was particularly helpful in the case of *Breastfeeding Made Simple* was that she was also a new mother. She read our book when her daughter was only 5 months old, and her own experience was still fresh in her mind. She was not only an experienced editor; she was a member of our target audience.

We received 25 pages of queries from her about the book, which was a lot. But with every question, I knew that we were increasing our readability with the group we wanted to reach. In the end, Honeychurch and Tesilya Hanauer (our acquisitions editor) went to the production department and got them to use a larger font so that the text would be more readable for sleep-deprived new moms. That was no mean feat. It raised the price of the book but was worth it in the end because the book looked better and would better meet the needs of our audience. Honeychurch explained it this way: "Your editor, if she believes in you and the book, can be your best ally and advocate when dealing with the publisher.

Editors can get things done that the writer may not even know need doing."

My relationships with editors have not been all sunshine and song, however. When going through editing with one of my books, I knew I was in for a rough ride when by page 2 of my manuscript, the editor asked me to define "pocket protector." Definitely not a good sign. In several places, she marked sentences with, "Is this a joke?" (Obviously a funny one!) It was a pain in the neck to read through page after page of queries like that. In the end, however, I must admit that many of the changes she made actually did make things better—and the rest I could live with.

Mistakes Authors Often Make

I basically see writers make two mistakes when it comes to working with editors: (a) They do everything, even if they disagree, or (b) they fight hand-to-hand combat over every comma. I remember once editing a book where one of the chapter authors told me "every word is precious." That obviously made my job more difficult. Acting like a diva will buy you nothing. But neither will being a doormat.

Treat your editors as part of the team. When you approach your relationship that way, you're apt to do things differently. You won't be afraid to speak up when you disagree. You are less likely to take feedback personally. When editors mark up your manuscript, they have one purpose: to make the writing better

(Bly, 2005; Glatzer, 2005b). It's not to make you cry. And if you want a good working relationship with your editors, I'd also advise you to avoid the actions that editors hate.

Things That Editors Hate

Having been both an author and an editor, I'm amazed at some of the stunts that authors will pull. Because I've been on both sides of the table, I've also been called in to mediate some disputes. Through these experiences, I've gleaned some ideas about behaviors that will derail your relationship with your editor, possibly even limiting your ability to do any future work with them.

Going Over Word or Page Limits

The first thing editors hate is when academic writers go over word or page limits. "It will take as many pages as it takes," is frequently our rallying cry. Unfortunately, most publishers won't accept this attitude. Editors often have very strict parameters within which they need to work. They can't afford to let you just go on and on. If they ask for a 1,500-word article on a topic, don't give them 3,000 or 4,500 words and expect them to love you for it. They won't. Magazines also have strict limits on how many inches of text they can fit in an issue. With book publishers, your page limit will be the upper limit of pages they can produce and sell within a certain price range. If authors produce more pages than that, the book will make less money per copy. Although some academic houses may be more flexible with page limits, the majority of them have the same financial bottom lines as trade houses and will expect you to deliver your manuscript at the contracted length.

Sometimes, length is negotiable. If you realize during the writing process that you are running long, you may be able to get more space. But talk with your editor sooner rather than later—and not the day before it's due (Glatzer, 2005a), or worse, after you've turned it in. See whether you and your editor can reach an agreement you both can live with.

Blowing off Deadlines

Academics have a horrible reputation among editors for blowing off deadlines—deservedly so. Let me say this as nicely as possible: If you approach your writing assignments with this attitude, you are headed for trouble. Editors, particularly of periodicals, have to have material ready to print on a regular basis. If you promise to get an article to them by July 25, you'd better have it to them by July 25. If you are writing for a magazine or newsletter, they're reserving space for you. After they receive all of the promised articles, the articles need to be formatted, copyedited, and printed. Each of these steps takes place on a tight production schedule. When you are late, you mess up the whole process.

Book publishers also have fairly tight schedules that they must adhere to. Once they receive your manuscript, it must be copyedited and sent to production for layout. Marketing will begin to work on selling your book, often months before you have finished the manuscript. If you miss your deadline by weeks or months, then your article or book may not be accepted for production at all, or you will delay or halt the whole production cycle.

When your manuscript finally arrives, there may not be anyone available to edit it, because the editorial team has moved on to other projects. Book buyers may no longer be interested, because they thought it was available at one time only to be told that it wasn't. So unless you're really famous, do whatever you can to meet your deadlines. That being said, if you've had a major crisis, such as catastrophic illness, you can usually work something out. But call your editor. I'd do that even if you are famous, because it's the polite thing to do.

TYPES OF EDITORS

Not everyone who wears the editor's hat has the same function within a publishing house. There are different types of editors. When I understood this and what each of their roles were, I found it easier to go through the process. The types of editors I describe here are ones you will typically encounter when writing books.

But editors for magazines and other periodicals may have similar titles and roles.

Acquisitions Editors

When you first approached your publisher, the person you most likely spoke with was the acquisitions editor. These are editors in charge of acquiring new works for their publisher. Sometimes acquisitions editors even approach potential authors with a book idea. New Harbinger Publications, for example, markets self-help mental health books. Their target audience is mental health practitioners and the general public. When acquiring new works, the acquisitions editors may approach a speaker at a professional meeting if they think that the speaker has an interesting take on a problem. They will also scour lists of professional publications to see whether any of these might work as a self-help book. Finally, they will review inquiries from the field when potential authors communicate with them about ideas they have for possible books. Many publishers have author guidelines on their Web sites, so authors can determine whether their book idea might be a good match for them.

Going through the acquisitions process can take weeks or months. It is rare to have someone buy your idea on the first go-round, especially when you are a beginning author. You may need to send your book idea back and forth a few times. I first pitched my book, *The Well-Ordered Home* (Kendall-Tackett, 2003), in a two-sentence e-mail, but it ended up having a fairly lengthy acquisitions process.

My original conceptualization was to write a short book (about 100 pages), broken down into seven chapters, on how to take care of your home. The publisher didn't immediately see how this book related to their list. My credentials as a psychologist helped. But the clincher was my making the connection between mess and stress. This was a book that helped people deal with stress by keeping their surroundings more orderly.

We still had to nail down the format it should take. We both agreed on the length (about 100 pages), and we agreed that it should be formatted as a "gift book." But we went back and forth about how best to arrange the chapters. They had recently published a couple of titles with 50 two-page chapters, and my editor thought this would be a good way to frame my material as well.

My next step was to come up with 50 chapter titles. That was a little more challenging. I sent in a list of titles. They liked most of them but had questions about a few. While my editor and I were going back and forth, she was also going back and forth with her marketing team. They also had ideas that my editor was forwarding to me.

The next task for us was to come up with an organizing framework. For the outline that was finally accepted, I grouped similar tasks together, but I really didn't have a good handle on the overall organization until I sat down to pull the whole manuscript together.

When doing this, I realized that there were four basic rules to household organization. Once I had a handle on those, I organized all the chapters around those four rules.

Developmental Editors

Developmental editors are those who review your work—typically a book manuscript—while it is still formative and provide feedback. Some developmental editors will review a few chapters to see whether they are on target in terms of content, style, and presentation. Others prefer to see a full draft manuscript so they can gauge how the book as a whole hangs together. Not every publisher offers developmental editing, but it can be helpful, especially if you are a first-time author, to have your work reviewed in this way.

Books almost always evolve in unexpected ways while you are writing. But you don't want the final product to be a huge surprise to your editors. The developmental edit can keep that from happening. During a developmental edit, you can expect edits that are broad in scope rather than line-by-line editing.

A developmental editor may also send material out for peer review. I've had this happen with several books I either edited or authored. Some publishers generally only do development on a full manuscript, although sometimes they will offer comments on individual draft chapters. This is because it is difficult to provide broad-stroke feedback without being able to see how the manuscript works as a whole. Most of these changes are to content, not typos or line edits. And you don't need to make every change that is marked. I remember one comment, in particular, that was so off-the-wall that I didn't know how to respond. The book was about women's stress and trauma, and the reviewer said that we had focused too much on women! (I believe that "huh?" was my pithy reply.) I happily got permission to ignore that comment.

Keep in mind that you don't need to go lockstep through every change your editor suggests. When I was working on the first edition of *The Hidden Feelings of Motherhood* (Kendall-Tackett, 2001), I received some feedback with which I disagreed. After reading the first three chapters, the editor told me to make the text "hard hitting and edgy" to differentiate my book from other parenting books. Hard hitting and edgy seemed like the wrong approach to me. It would have differentiated the book all right, but not in a good way. Just to be sure, I ran these comments by some colleagues. Just as I suspected, the universal reply was "What?!" I went back to the editor and respectfully pointed out that hard hitting and edgy was the wrong direction. They agreed and let me write it the way I wanted to.

A developmental edit has advantages and challenges. One advantage is that it breaks your job into smaller components and gives you some concrete goals to shoot for, which can be a great incentive to get going. Some publishers may have you send in a few chapters at a time. Others may want half of the manuscript.

For me, one of the challenges of a developmental edit is having to produce part of a book independent of all the other parts. Books change as I work on them. The basic content is generally the same, but I move things all over the place. If you are asked to turn in your manuscript in sections, find out if you will be able to edit those sections once you turn them in. I once worked with the author of one of the "Dummies" books. In that series, the publishers find experts on a topic and have them draft the material. These experts aren't necessarily writers, however. As the authors turn in chapters, the publishers have a ghostwriter rework the prose, put it into their format, and add humor. But once chapters are turned in, the authors listed on the cover aren't allowed to touch them again. The author with whom I worked had actually wanted to make a structural change. As she was writing, she found a framework that helped her to organize the rest of the book. She wanted to apply it to the part she had already turned in. She eventually prevailed, but it practically took an act of Congress to get the chapters back. So be sure to find out whether you can reedit sections before you sign an agreement.

Copy (or Line) Editors

Once you have successfully completed your manuscript, you will submit it to the acquisitions or development editor, who will then hand it off to a copy editor. Copy editors perform the task that most people think of as "editing." They focus on things like flow and logic, ask you for references if the text seems to warrant them, check all of your references, and generally try to clean up your manuscript (Niles, 2005). They may point out that what you've said in one part of your manuscript contradicts something you say later.

Your part in the copyediting phase typically takes anywhere from 1 to 2 weeks—a figure that surprises many first-time authors. Before scheduling your copyedits, you may get an e-mail or call asking if you'd be available to receive edits during a certain week. Although it won't take all of your time during the allotted 2 weeks, it can take a substantial amount. It's also very important that you review the edits and send them back by the deadline. If you are late, your publisher may have difficulty scheduling the production of your manuscript. This can delay publication substantially.

When it's copyediting time, you will receive a copy of your manuscript with the editor's marks. Some publishers will send you pages that have already been typeset to edit. Others will send back copies of your original manuscript. Don't be shocked if your beloved manuscript has lots and lots of marks. It doesn't mean that it was bad. Your editor is simply being thorough. Take a deep breath and start plowing through the edits.

I've found that it is better for me to review the edits in smaller batches, because my eyes glaze over after awhile. It's best if you can read the edits while you are fresh. That's one of the reasons why it is good to set aside enough time to give them a thorough read. I tend to review the edited manuscript several times just to make sure it reads the way I want it to.

There will be several types of marks. The first will be editing of the text. Your editor will find typos and mark them as well as any punctuation or usage errors. The text editing is especially important if you are someone who misses your own typos. I am. It's always easier for me to edit someone else's copy because my mind doesn't know what's supposed to be there. Your editor may also make changes in pagination or where a paragraph breaks.

Your copy editor may also suggest headers. Read the headers over carefully. I recently had a magazine editor unknowingly put things under the wrong header level in an article I had written. I was describing the conditions that co-occur with postpartum depression. "Comorbid Conditions" was supposed to be the A-level header, with each of the types as subheads under this general header (PTSD, Anxiety, Eating Disorders, etc.). Unfortunately, somewhere in the copyediting phase, all of these subcategories ended up as separate A-level headers, which communicated something different than if these were types of comorbid conditions. It wasn't the end of the world, but it did change the meaning (Kendall-Tackett, 2005d).

Your copy editor will also mark things for the typesetter, such as type of font and levels of headers.

Finally, your copy editor will mark anything that isn't clear.

With most publishers, you are offered these edits for your approval. Start with your first page and read through every one. Most of the time, you'll agree with the edits. Some edits won't really change things one way or the other. If you can live with the change, leave it alone. If you think it changes meaning, however, speak up. In almost every case, I've had the editor agree to put things back the way they were or approve a new wording of the text. You can make some marks right on the page, or if the change is longer, mark it on a letter to the copy editor that you will send back with your manuscript.

Copy editors may also mark usage of certain words. In English, there is a move to get rid of hyphens wherever possible by joining two words that are always used together. For example, in the lactation field, we used to talk about mothers as *breast feeding* (or *bottle feeding*). Then it became *breast-feeding*. This is the way it is listed in the dictionary and is still used in many medical journals (important to keep in mind for Medline searches). However, in the lactation field, the preferred spelling is now one word: *breastfeeding*.

Whenever I review for one of the lactation journals, and I see "breast-feeding" in the text, I know that the author is not in the field. That's a little background on a usage skirmish I recently had over copyediting of my book, *Depression in New Mothers* (Kendall-Tackett, 2005a). That book is geared toward the lactation community in that every treatment option I described has been framed in terms of how it impacts breastfeeding. So imagine my shock when I opened my copyedited manuscript and saw that the diligent copy editor had changed every *breastfeeding* to *breast-feeding*. I used that word about 200 times. I immediately wrote to the editor and said that she needed to change it back because it would make me look like an amateur if we left it hyphenated. I marked it every place I saw it, but I also asked her to do a search. She promised to fix it, and she did.

Edits are either electronic or in pencil on hard copy. Hard copy edits are becoming less common, and you are likely to receive electronic files with changes marked or hard copies with electronic changes showing in text. Some editors will ask for you to make any requested changes in red so they can see them easily. Other editors may want you to mark changes in pencil. The cover letter that comes with your copyedited manuscript will generally have specific instructions. So read that before you dive in. For longer changes, the editor will typically ask for you to type the edits, attach the typed page, and enclose a diskette or CD with all of the longer edits in electronic format.

This procedure may be changing soon. With my most recent manuscript, the copyediting phase was completed electronically. The copy editor marked the changes using the "track changes" function of MS Word and e-mailed the chapters to me in batches of three or four at a time. I reviewed the changes (which were fortunately small) and sent the files back. I also marked electronically anything on which I had a question or wanted to change back.

Production Editors

This is the last place where your manuscript goes before your publisher sends it to the printer. For some publishers, the copy and production editor functions are handled by the same person. If separate, the production editor is responsible for overseeing the typesetting of your manuscript and the design of your page layout.

At this phase, there may also be some queries for you to answer. The production editor may have spotted some new typos (it's always good to have someone else take a look at your manuscript). There may also be references to check. Mainly, what the production editor does is decide how things will look on the page. They will look at pagination and white space; format of tables, figures, and photos; and where chapter and section headers go.

RESPONDING TO EDITS

No matter how good the book or article, someone, somewhere is going to have a problem with it. Sometimes knowing that even literary masterpieces have been criticized can provide much-needed perspective when you receive comments from others. I just read something the other day where a new author wondered how Jane Austen ever got published. Let's see if his book is still in print in 200 years! Even one of the biggest selling books of the 20th century, *The Lord of the Rings* (J. R. R. Tolkien, 1954 and 1955/2002), had its detractors. When the first installment of the movie version was about to be released, I saw a documentary about Tolkien. A member of his writers' group would (apparently) repeatedly say, "Please, no more dwarves, elves, and hobbits." Apparently, not a huge fan of Middle Earth.

There may be times when you receive overly critical comments from either an editor or a reviewer. I wish I could spare you from this experience, because it really isn't fun. I hope you will take comfort in knowing that most of us go through this. And how you respond to nasty comments is what separates the pros from the wannabes. Author Jenna Glatzer (2005b) wrote about how even though she's been through this process several different times, it always comes as a shock when she receives the marked-up pages from her editor. She recommended the following strategies for coping:

- *Find a fume friend.* Call someone for social support. I have a couple of friends with whom I can share my negative reviews. Just having someone else to read these types of comments can help you cope. Ideally, this person is someone who loves you unconditionally and tells you your work is pure genius. If you don't have a friend like that, find one.

Or you could consider an online or an in-person writers' group.

- *Back away from your manuscript.* Don't try to address changes while you are still reeling from shock. Give yourself at least 24 hours before you tackle the first query. If the comments are really bad, give yourself anywhere from a week to a month to deal with them. But don't go longer than that. It's important that you don't let negative remarks permanently derail your work. And if you wait longer than a month, you may be tempted to never finish that project.

- *Know that red ink means she cares.* A marked up manuscript means your editor has carefully gone over things for the sole purpose of making it better. Editing takes time—a lot of time, much of which is thankless. Try to keep that in mind as you read.

- *Start with simple changes.* Just as when you are writing a first draft, you don't need to tackle every question in order. Pick out the easy ones first, which will give you a sense of accomplishment that will sustain you as you tackle more difficult comments.

- *Prioritize arguments.* Basically, this suggestion means you should pick your battles. Not every change is of equal importance. Fighting over every comma marks you as an amateur. And I've found a lot of individual differences when it comes to commas, use of contractions, and style. Honestly,

I don't care that much about things like commas. I put them in where I think they go, but don't have a heart attack when they get taken out or moved. Ditto with contractions. I've had some editors go through and take out every contraction I've made in the text, and other editors who suggest I add more. That's another thing I don't tend to worry about unless it substantially changes the flow of a passage.

- *Compromise.* Try to compromise if you can. This is where prioritizing your arguments is crucial. Can you make the changes you care less about in order to keep the other sections unchanged? Identify the changes you can't live with and fight for those. If they are less crucial, you can be flexible. Almost always there is a way for you and your editor to work well together.

GALLEY EDITS

Not all publishers do this, but some will let you have one last shot at your manuscript before it goes to the printer. During this phase, your publisher may send you typeset pages for a final review. Find out if you will be able to edit at this time, because it can influence how thorough you need to be. Even if you get to review galleys, not all publishers will allow you to make substantive changes at this point. Your publisher will then proofread the galleys one last time before sending them to the printer.

Conclusion

Working with editors can occupy a significant amount of your writing time, and not always pleasantly. As difficult as editing can sometimes be, it is well worth the effort. In almost all cases, editors will improve your writing. Try your best not to take comments personally, get support when you need it, and don't be afraid to speak up when you disagree. You and your editor are working toward the same goal: making you look good and getting your words out before the public.

8

Writing Articles for Magazines, Newsletters, and Web Sites

I decided to write for a general audience because the work I was doing—the topics, that is—had some popular appeal and could be useful to people.
—Mike Mangan

Writing articles for magazines, newsletters, and Web sites can dramatically increase the number of people reading your work. It is often said that only five people read the average journal article. Of course, it really depends on the article. But for many, the readership is generally small. What if you could take what was in that journal article and repackage it so people outside your field could understand its significance? Although that won't work for every topic, it will work for more than you think. In this chapter, I'll review the basics of writing for newsletters, magazines, and Web sites, starting with print publications.

Writing for Newsletters and Magazines

Writing for newsletters or magazines can be a great way for you to break into writing for a general audience. In this type of writing, you use a more conversational tone than you would for journal articles or book chapters. You can also use some of the storytelling techniques I described in chapter 4. Even telling a story about a study can be effective. What were you looking for? How did you conduct the study? What did you find? Why is it relevant to the reader? Show the reader why the finding is interesting and why it matters.

How to Select a Publication

One of your first tasks is to select the newsletter or magazine that you want to write for. With thousands of publications available, it can be difficult and overwhelming to know where to start. Below are some suggestions.

Start With What You Read

A natural place for you to begin your search is with publications that you already read. Are there magazines or newsletters for your professional organizations? You could also start with any alumni magazines that you receive. These publications are often looking for good material and can give you some experience with article writing. Before you query a publication, make sure the information, especially the editor's name, is accurate by looking at a current issue of the publication, visiting the Web site, or making a quick phone call to the editorial office.

Writer's Market

If you plan to pursue magazine articles, one resource that you absolutely need is a current edition of *Writer's Market*. This publication lists magazine and book publishers, divides them by topics they specialize in, and has contact information for editors. It also tells a bit about the publications, such as how much they pay and the terms of a typical agreement.

Many of the periodicals I write for are not listed in *Writer's Market*, because they are small and specialized publications. But most of the larger publishers are listed, and it's a good resource to have. I actually prefer the online version of *Writer's Market* because it is searchable (http://www.writersmarket.com). *Writer's Digest* Book Club usually offers *Writer's Market* at a good price if you want a hard copy (http://www.writers digestbookclub.com).

What to Know About the Publication

As you read over the listings of possible publications, try to get a feel for the articles they publish. What topics seem to come up a lot? What type of format do they tend to use (e.g., do they publish articles that describe "10 tips to . . .")? Do they like articles that summarize current research? Do they describe people's experiences? Do they prefer articles written in the first person or third person? What is the general tone of the articles? Do they include pictures? What is the average length of articles?

If there are regular columns, would your article fit into a particular one? It may be better to query the editor of that column rather than the editor-in-chief. Finally, keep in mind seasonal deadlines. Magazine editors usually work about 8 to 9 months out. So if you have an idea for a Christmas article, for example, you'll want to pitch it in March or April. Similarly, summer articles usually need to be pitched in October (Tank, 2005). Newsletters generally have shorter lead times, but even these can be 3 to 4 months out.

In addition, try to get a feel for the audience who reads the publication. If it's one that you read, then you will already have a good sense of who they are. If it is not a publication with which you are familiar, educate yourself about who the audience is and what they need from you. There's no substitute for doing your homework. Editor David Tank (2005) told authors to read the publication to get a sense of what the editors want. In each issue, editors lay out their preferences for all the world to see:

> It's the first thing every budding writer should learn. Yet I am continually mystified by the number of manuscripts I receive from folks who apparently have never laid eyes on my magazine. . . . Let me say it one more time: If you want to read an editor's mind, you need to carefully read the editor's publication. (pp. 49–50)

Author Guidelines

The next piece of information you need are the author guidelines. These are usually found on the publication's Web site. The author guidelines for magazines are similar to author guidelines for journals. These guidelines will tell you about the mechanics of publication: length of the average article, where to send it, how to submit it. But, as Tank (2005) pointed out, the author guidelines are no substitute for reading the publication; the guidelines will not give you any information about a publication's "soul."

Writing a Query Letter

After identifying your topic, audience, and publication, your next step is to contact the editor to see if he or she is interested in your idea. Not too long ago, this was all done by letter, via regular mail. If you sent out a lot of letters, querying editors could be costly and time consuming. Fortunately, the day of the e-query is here. For many publications, you e-mail an editor to introduce yourself and pitch an article idea.

As with anything else, there is an art to writing a query letter. You want to sound interesting without being corny or slick. And you don't want to sound like a braggart. In my experience, the query process for newsletters tends to be less formal than for a magazine. Often my query will be something along the lines of, "I have an idea for an article. What do you think?" The editor and I will frequently go back and forth a few times as we reach an agreement on focus, word count, and deadline. If interested, the editor will usually assign me a deadline and word count. Newsletter articles tend to be short: about 700 to 850 words. (One manuscript page is approximately 250 words.) Sometimes, they are even shorter than that. You must be able to summarize your thoughts concisely and in a way that grabs your readers. I usually start with more words than I need and trim them down. But I try not to go too far over my limit because editing excess words can be quite time consuming.

Sample Query

I have to admit, I've never gotten good at the slick query letter. Whenever I try to come up with one, my efforts just fall flat. I tend to be straightforward when I communicate. So that's the approach I use when querying editors. Below is an e-query I might send. Let's say I want to write for a magazine called *Natural Parent* and the editor's name is Mara Simpson.

Dear Ms. Simpson:

My name is Kathleen Kendall-Tackett. I am a psychologist and lactation consultant. I am on the research faculty at the University of New Hampshire and have authored or edited 15 books on topics related to women's health, including *Depression in New Mothers* and *The Hidden Feelings of Motherhood*. I'm writing to propose two possible articles for *Natural Parent*.

The first is on alternative and complementary treatments for depression. This topic has been very much in the news with the recent dialog between Tom Cruise and Brooke Shields on whether medications are necessary for the treatment of depression. In some cases, medications are necessary. But there is exciting new research showing the efficacy of the treatments using exercise, omega-3s, and herbs.

The second topic is on some of the new thinking about depression in new mothers. Researchers are now looking more holistically at how factors such as fatigue, stress, and the immune system all play a role. Plus, we now know much more about how a difficult birth can cause psychological trauma and trigger an episode of depression.

I have attached some recent articles I have published on similar topics. I propose that these articles be 1,500 words in length, but I am flexible on word count.

Thank you for your consideration. I look forward to hearing from you.

Sincerely,

Kathleen Kendall-Tackett, PhD, IBCLC

Let's go step-by-step through this query, starting with the salutation.

Salutation. One thing you must do is accurately specify the editor's name. You can get this from *Writer's Market* (if it's a larger publication) or from the publisher's masthead. If you are not certain of the editor's gender because he or she has a gender-neutral or gender-ambiguous name, don't guess. Either call the publication and find out, or write out their full name (Dear Mara Simpson vs. Dear Ms. Simpson).

Credentials. The next thing I did was to specify my credentials as they related to her publication. I am a lactation consultant. I specified this because the editor is as well, and her magazine focuses on many related issues.

In the next sentence, I established my academic credentials, which are important because *Natural Parent* likes articles with an empirical base. So I let her know that my work would be evidence based and that I have written extensively on the topics that I was proposing. I also have written two books that are directly relevant to the topic at hand. That information is important both for the editor and for readers.

Then I wrote brief synopses of articles I could write. In the first one, I directly tied into an event that had been in the news. Actress Brooke Shields had gone public with her story of severe postpartum depression. As part of her recovery, she took antidepressant medications. Actor Tom Cruise, a noted expert on treatment options for depression (NOT!), publicly stated that she did not need to be on medications. By the time you read this book, this story will be old news. Brooke and Tom are friends now. However, it is often a good idea to relate your intended article idea to relevant current events, because providing a hook with a recent event will make your article more relevant to readers. In this case, readers may be wondering whether there are alternatives to antidepressants. This will especially be an issue for the readers of *Natural Parent*, who are also interested in natural health and alternative medicine.

The second proposed article described some of the latest thinking about depression in new mothers. Although past research has focused on things like shifts in reproductive hormone levels (e.g., estrogen and progesterone), we're now finding out that the immune system plays a much greater role than we imagined. This helps explain why anti-inflammatory omega-3s would have an impact on depression—just one of the areas where thinking about depression has changed. If I were to write this article, I'd describe some others as well.

Word Count. As for word count, I proposed 1,500 words (about six manuscript pages) but indicated that I was flexible about that. These articles could range anywhere from 800 to 2,500 words, depending on what the editor needed. So I indicated that I would work with her to find the size of article she needed to fit within an issue. If I had some suggested sidebars, I might include these as well. Two possible sidebars for the articles I proposed are "Symptoms of Depression" and "Where to Go for Additional Help."

Clips. Finally, I told the editor that I was attaching some clips of recent articles. (*Clips* are reprints of articles you've written.) The first article was one I wrote for mothers titled, "Making Peace With Your Birth Experience" (Kendall-Tackett, 2002). In it, I described how a difficult birth can cause psychological trauma and depression, and I offered women some specific suggestions about what they can do to cope.

The second article, from a publication for people who work with new moms, was titled, "New Research in Postpartum Depression" (Kendall-Tackett, 2005d).

With that, I signed off and thanked her for her consideration. Some authors tell you to refer editors to your Web site (if you have one). Others think that this is the mark of an amateur. You can decide. What I have done is to list my three Web sites under my e-mail signature, so people can look at them if they want. When they do, they'll see more of my publications.

Providing What an Editor Needs

As an academic, your credentials allow you to skip past most of the hoi polloi in the editorial slush pile. But an academic title presents you with two distinct disadvantages. First, editors are often concerned about whether you can actually write at an accessible level for their publication. As I described in chapter 3, academics have the justified reputation of being long winded, which means more work for the editor, who may need to substantially edit your prose before it is ready for publication. Your second disadvantage is academics' casual disregard for deadlines.

You need to convince the editor that neither of these things will be true for you. And you can do that with your clips. When you present clips, you show the editor that you know how to write. You also show them that you've written before and know what is expected in terms of providing the article you promised in a timely manner. One editor in a recent *Writer's Digest* article (Glatzer, 2005a) said that she likes to see multiple clips from the same publication, if possible. That tells her that the author has an established relationship with an editor and is therefore probably easy to work with.

Related to this, editors may wonder whether you are going to be difficult to work with because of your advanced education. This is a realistic concern. When I was an undergraduate, I remember one of the new professors telling off a secretary because she fixed a minor punctuation error in a letter she was asked to type. The professor assumed that because he had a PhD, and the secretary did not, that he knew more than she did. What he didn't realize was that she had a BA in English and was working on her master's degree. She definitely knew more than he did about writing. His little outburst infuriated all of the secretaries and pretty much guaranteed that his work got last priority in their work queue for as long as he was there. Moral of the story: Acting like a jackass doesn't pay. Always treat editors like your colleagues. They may not have your advanced education, but chances are they know more than you do when it comes to producing workable prose.

As for word count, getting a good feel for how many words it will take to cover a topic sufficiently will come with practice (for further discussion, see chap. 10). If you really don't know how many words you will need, then consider drafting the article before you pitch the idea. It doesn't need to be in final form to estimate how many words it will be.

As much as possible, adhere to your agreed-on word count. If you are going over the word count, then contact your editor and tell him or her. As one editor explained to *Writer's Digest* (Glatzer, 2005a), it's better to know that information sooner rather than later. Your editor may be able to give you more space. Or they may have some suggestions about how you can cut things down by shifting your focus.

Types of Assignments

So you've written a dazzling query and the editor is interested. What next? If you are writing for a smaller publication, chances are the editor will tell you to go ahead and write the article. The editor will usually give you a word count and deadline, and you can correspond with him or her if you have questions. If you are going to be paid, then the editor will usually discuss payment with you up front.

Another way you might get assigned an article is "on spec." This means that the editor has agreed to read your finished article but is not guaranteeing that it will be published (Glatzer, 2005c). This is obviously not ideal for you. But sometimes, it's the only way to get an editor to take a chance on you, an unproven author. Before agreeing to this type of assignment, find out whether there is a "kill fee," a fee that they pay in the event that they don't use your work. Even if an editor decides not to use your work, chances are someone else will take it. I would also recommend that you don't assign them your copyright until they agree to publish it. You don't want your article hung up for months when you can't take it elsewhere.

The final type of assignment is when the editor agrees to pay you for the article. Payment could be a flat fee or, more commonly, by the word. Often the terms of payment are specified in *Writer's Market*, but there is frequently a range of payment. When you are just starting out, you will probably be on the low side of the pay range. With experience, you will be able to receive more money for your work.

Fair warning: Most small publications will pay only a small fee, if any, for your work. But there are still good reasons to write for them. (a) It's a way to get some experience and clips for your portfolio, (b) it's good practice, (c) it can help you break into a new field, and (d) it gives you a way to support a cause that you care about (Hayden, 2005; Notbohm, 2006).

Assignment of Copyright

Many small publications will not have you sign a copyright agreement, so you retain the copyright to your material. For larger publications, you may have to sign a copyright agreement that assigns "first serial rights" to the publisher (Feiertag & Cupito, 2004). If you sign one of these, it means that the publisher has the right to publish your article first. But then you can sell that same article to another publication that buys "second serial rights" (Feiertag & Cupito, 2004). Many freelance writers do this routinely as a great way to continue generating revenue from research and writing they've already done. In fact, you may find that it helps to have a library of clips. That way, when you get inspired to write about a particular issue, you can pull from something you have already written and adapt it for a current article, providing that you have retained the rights to the material. That saves a lot of time.

A copyright agreement that assigns "all rights" to the publisher is the most restrictive for authors. It means that the publication owns first and second serial rights and also rights to your article in other forms, including the electronic rights. If a publisher owns the electronic rights, you can't post your article on your Web site without permission.

Agreements that assign all rights to the publisher are obviously the least beneficial to you, but you may have to sign this type of agreement in order to get your work published. Only you can decide if that is a fair trade. Usually, it is.

Writing for newsletters and magazines is a great way to get your work before a wider audience. This type of writing starts when you identify a publication you want to write for and contact the editor. Ideally, you'll establish ongoing relationships with editors you write for, and these relationships can lead to even more opportunities. I interviewed one author who

154

has successfully established such relationships; see Exhibit 8.1.

WRITING FOR THE WORLD WIDE WEB

Although the Internet has not replaced print media the way some expected, eventually we may see Web publications eclipse their print brethren. The Internet is increasingly becoming the media of choice for the next generation and is changing the way we get information.

As I write this, the Internet is still in its adolescence. But opportunities abound for writers of clear prose on the Web. In describing this vacuum, Michael Meanwell (2004) described how a growing number of businesses are reevaluating their content and trying to make it accessible for visitors to the site. And that's where writers come in.

As an academic author, you may not be interested in writing content for just any Web site. But you can write content for organizations you care about, or to promote a book, or to make your work more accessible to readers.

I have quite a few articles published on the Web, between my own sites and the sites of organizations I have written for. The potential reach of these articles is enormous. As I mentioned earlier, the average academic article has a relatively small number of readers. In contrast, Web sites can have millions of readers.

EXHIBIT 8.1 Profile of a Magazine Author

Teresa Pitman writes full time for Canada's largest parenting magazine, *Today's Parent*. I asked her some questions about how she got started and what type of work she does.

Tell me about the magazine you got started writing for. Who's the audience? Do you write a column?

I actually started out writing for a magazine called *Great Expectations*, a magazine about pregnancy and birth for Canadian parents. The company that published that magazine also publishes *Today's Parent*, and after several years, I was invited to do some articles for them.

I have a column. The articles focus on developmental or behavioral issues that come up with specific age groups. I love writing these, and all the reader surveys they have done say that it is the most popular section in the magazine. I also write feature articles for *Today's Parent* and on occasion for other publications.

How did you get started writing for *Today's Parent*? Did you start as a freelancer? Do you still freelance, too?

I had written some fiction and won a couple of short story contests, and I had some children's fiction published (in school textbooks). Two of my friends had decided to start up a mail order book business and asked me if I would write some book reviews for their catalogue. The editor of *Pregnancy and Birth* saw the catalogue and called up my friend to ask who had written the book reviews. Then she called me and asked if I would be interested in writing for the magazine. That was the beginning.

I am still considered a freelancer with the magazine, and in addition do a variety of other freelance writing. Besides the magazine work, I write a newspaper column and write for various organizations. For example, I recently finished a project for the Hospital for Sick Children in Toronto and one for the

continued

156

EXHIBIT 8.1 *Continued*

Peel Region Children's Aid Society. And of course, I write books (Number 12 was recently published, although it was ghostwritten so my name isn't on it. And I'm working on Number 13).

What have been some of your biggest challenges in doing this type of writing?

For me, writing usually comes fairly easily. The research can be more challenging. Usually, if I suggest an article, I have in mind some people to interview. But many of my articles are written about topics that the editors have come up with on their own and ask me to do. And it is not always as easy for me to find people for those! It is sometimes harder to find parents whose experiences with their children fit into the article.

Even my own Web site has about 13,000 visitors each month. By cyberspace standards, that's small. But compared with the usual number of journal article readers, it's huge.

Freelance writer Michael Meanwell (2004) has identified several potential markets for those interested in writing for Web sites:

■ *Articles written for print publications.* Depending on the agreement you have with your publisher, articles you've written for a print newsletter or magazine may also end up on the Web. If you have your own Web site, ask whether the publisher's Web site can put a link to your Web site or whether you can have the electronic version of your article available on your site.

- *Short articles written for the site.* You may also write new material for a site, particularly if you have expertise in an area. One author I know has written several articles based on her books that she offers for free to Web sites. It's great advertising for her books, and she is providing genuinely helpful information.

- *Online courses.* E-learning is the wave of the future and offers another great opportunity for you to educate your colleagues without having to travel. I've had two of my continuing educational modules be turned into online continuing education for health care providers. Providers can read the module, take the posttest, and receive credits online. I was paid for those modules, and they have also led to some speaking engagements and consulting work.

Tips for Writing on the Web

Readers of Web sites have different needs than readers of print material. For example, people tend to read computer screens somewhat more slowly than they do hard copy. Meanwell (2004) recommended that you write about half as much as you usually would for an article. If you need to provide more content, use hyperlinks to other pages.

As is true for print publications, headers and subheaders help readers scan information and find what they need. Headers also visually break up a page and encourage the reader to keep reading. Bullet points are also helpful for readers who may be looking for specific information, as are lists and pull-out quotes. You can also summarize a page's content at the top of each page to help readers determine whether they want to keep reading.

As for style, similar rules apply both to online content and to print. Write in a conversational tone, using an active voice. Present only one idea in each paragraph, and realize that paragraphs may be read out of order, depending on where readers land after searching for specific information. Do your paragraphs have enough information so that they could be read alone? Finally, remember that your readers are from all over the world. English is the official language of high tech. But there are substantial differences in how English is used in different countries, so be aware of the differences I described in chapter 6. Although you don't want to lose your unique voice, try to write with the needs of readers from other countries in mind.

Pitching an Idea

Pitching a Web article idea is similar to pitching an article for a print publication. If it is an e-zine, find out the name of the editor, and send him or her an e-mail query. This should be like the queries you would send to a print publication. Spiegel (2005) suggested that you do not attach article clips, because the editor's system may discard attachments from unknown writers. As an alternative, he suggested that you paste a paragraph from several relevant articles at the end of your e-mail, telling the editor that you can furnish the full article on request. Or you could have your clips online and refer the editor to your site by providing a link or the URL.

Finding an online editor's contact information can sometimes be a challenge. You can usually find this information on the publication's Web site. If you are not sure which editor to send your query to, send it to the managing editor and ask that your query be forwarded to the appropriate person. For smaller sites, you can often simply contact the webmaster. Look for "Contact us" information for where to send your query. Smaller sites probably won't pay, but they are often thrilled to get articles that they don't have to write themselves. And writing these articles gives you experience publishing in this medium.

The 2005 *Writer's Market* (Brogan, 2005) does not have a separate listing for electronic publishers, but that is likely to change with future editions. *Writer's Market* can give you contact information for editors of print publications. If you can't find information about editors online, the *Writer's Market* listing can be a great place to start because many magazines also have online versions.

One caution is in order, however. If you publish something electronically, some print publishers won't touch it because it was "already published," even if it is only on your Web site. We ran into this at the lab where I work. Our director wanted to make "in press" articles available on the Web. We found out that by doing so, the authors would be violating their copyright agreement by publishing it first elsewhere. It's important to check before posting an article.

Conclusion

Writing articles for general-audience publications can be a wonderful experience. You will expand your reach well beyond the average readership of journal articles and provide useful information. As an author, you need to know the publication before you attempt to write for it. And you'll need to provide editors with clear prose, by your deadline and within your word limit. Remember to treat your editors like the colleagues they are. Having good working relationships with magazine, newsletter, and Web editors can lead to even more writing opportunities that will continue to get your work before an audience.

9

Selling Your Book Idea:
How to Find a Publisher

The profession of book writing makes horse racing
seem like a solid, stable business.
—*John Steinbeck (quoted in Rubie, 2003)*

Having looked in the previous chapter at how to write short articles of various kinds, let's focus now on the more complex task of getting a book published. Writing a book can be both thrilling and terrifying. And if you're new to the process, it can be hard to know where to begin. I prefer to have a book contract before I begin a large project like writing a book. Other authors like to write first, shop for a publisher second. Either way will work. And the process for finding a publisher for your manuscript is the same. In the next three chapters, I'll walk you through the process of finding a publisher, making a pitch, writing a proposal, and negotiating a contract. We'll begin with finding a publisher.

How to Select a Publisher

Entire books have been written about how to find a publisher. How do you know which one is right for you? Sometimes, the correct answer is "whoever is willing to publish my book." But your choice of publisher can make a big difference in terms of how your book is produced and marketed. In this section, I'll summarize the major types of publishers and help you think through the criteria that are important to you.

Selection Criteria

Over the years, I've found a few things that make a difference in terms of whether a publisher is a good match for my work. If you are not already familiar with the publisher, a little research will make a significant difference in how well you understand what they do and how they approach their work.

Similar Titles

The first question I ask when surveying a potential publisher is whether they publish titles similar to the one I'm proposing. This is important because they will have a much better idea of how to market your book if they are selling similar books. For example, when New Harbinger decided to publish *Breastfeeding Made Simple* (Mohrbacher & Kendall-Tackett, 2005), they had never published a breastfeeding book before. But they did publish parenting books. Some of those books, although not on the same topic, opened the door for our book, because New Harbinger's marketing team could sell our book along with the parenting books.

Often, when considering potential publishers, it helps to look on your own bookshelf. Who is publishing the types of books you read and want to write? That is often a good place for you to start looking for a publisher. Of course, that is no guarantee that they will publish your book. But it at least gives you a place to start.

Unagented Manuscripts

If you are just starting out in publishing, chances are that you don't have an agent representing you. That tends to be pretty typical among academics; often our books don't sell enough to attract an agent or to make sense for us to have one. But not having an agent can block you from potential publishers, especially the bigger houses.

When I was shopping for a publisher for a recent project, I explored three possible publishers. By doing a quick search, I learned that the largest (Little, Brown) did not accept unagented manuscripts. So I approached one of the smaller publishers. They offered my coauthor and me a contract, so I stopped the search there.

Not having an agent will limit the number of places where you can submit your manuscript. But it doesn't mean that no one will take it. Guidelines for authors listed on the company's Web site will tell you whether you need an agent in order to submit your proposal. If that information is not listed on the Web site, check their listing in *Writer's Market*. Don't be discouraged. Even without an agent, there are plenty of publishers who are willing to talk with you.

Production Quality

Something else to consider is the physical quality of the publisher's books. I look at paper quality, quality of binding, and quality of cover art. These things all make a difference in how readers perceive your book. You don't want someone to decide not to buy your book because it looks tacky.

Years ago, when I was book review editor for one of my professional organizations, I was struck by the garish covers that one publisher produced. I remember one book in particular with a neon yellow background with purple and green writing. The cover art looked like the poster girl from *Les Miserables* (picture that against neon yellow!). The final product was, in my opinion, ghastly. No way did I want one of my books to look like that. Fortunately, over the years, I noticed that their covers substantially improved. This publisher recently published one of my books, and the cover they produced was gorgeous. In fact, it is one of my favorites. So be sure to look at some of a publisher's more current titles.

Something else I look at is paper quality. A surprising number of books, mostly mass market, but even some trade books, are published on newsprint. Unfortunately, this type of paper does not age well; even after only a few years, it yellows and looks bad. When it is sitting around the warehouse, it's deteriorating and will probably be difficult to sell. That's bad news for you. Although I wouldn't necessarily say no to a publisher because of paper quality, it is something I'd consider. The only downside to nicer paper is that it weighs more. One of my books, in particular, is printed on very nice paper. But a box of books weighs almost 40 pounds. That's a lot of weight to try to lug through an airport. And the books cost more to ship.

Layout quality is another factor. How is the typesetting? Is it easy to read? Is there sufficient white space around the text? How do the pictures and illustrations look? Are they clear or do they look like a poor-quality mimeograph? Layout quality can also influence whether people decide to buy your book. If a book has text that runs out to the margins or seems inaccessible in other ways, buyers will most likely put it down and buy a different book.

The final thing I look at is binding quality. Do you really want to spend a year of your life writing a book with pages that fall out? Poor binding quality means that books get returned, which means fewer sales for you.

Length of Production Cycle

Another factor to consider is the length of a publisher's *production cycle*, or how long it takes from the time you turn your manuscript in to when it is ready to sell. Eight to 9 months is fairly typical, but I've had production cycles range from 2 months to 19 months. Ask a potential publisher this directly. If you know anyone who has published with them, ask them as well. The publisher may tell you a "typical" length of time assuming that everything runs like clockwork. But in many individual cases, the actual time may be quite a bit longer.

Although a long production cycle doesn't automatically rule out a publisher, it's better if you know it going in. One of my recent books took 19 months to go through production. That was frustrating because it was "in press" for so long. I had quite a few speaking engagements that would have been great places to sell the book. But all I could do was pass out flyers.

In the meantime, I had three other books that I started, finished, and went through production with and that were released before that one book came out. One of the editors at the tardy publisher tried to tell me that a 19-month production cycle was "typical." I was able to fire back with a well-documented au contraire, based on recent experience with three different publishers. The book did, eventually, come out. But I probably could have saved myself some angst if I had known about the long lead time from the beginning.

Backlist Sales

Something else for you to find out is how long the publishers keep books in print. You can get an idea about that by looking at their catalog or Web site. Do they still feature books that are a few years old? Older titles are known as a publisher's *backlist*. Over the life cycle of a book, backlist sales can be significant. Often, books will sell the most in the first few months after publication. But even after initial sales drop, year-after-year backlist sales can add up to significant numbers. So you may want to steer clear of publishers who seem to publish and then dump significant numbers of titles.

Types of Publishers

There are several types of publishers to choose from. When you are first starting out, you may need to work with smaller houses. But that is not always a bad thing. In fact, I prefer smaller publishers. Here's a brief description of types of publishers and the pros and cons of each.

Small Publishers

Small publishers are the fastest growing segment of the publishing world—with good reason. As more and more of the larger houses merge, small publishers meet a need for independent voices within the publishing community. Small publishers are also often more willing to publish edgy or unusual content (Niles, 2005).

Small publishers typically publish anywhere from 5 to 50 titles a year, and they often have a particular market niche. They will market your book well because they aren't releasing hundreds of titles a year. But don't expect flashy promotions from a small publisher, because they probably won't happen. And small publishers tend to offer smaller advances (if any). Further, they expect that you will work with them to promote your book, but this is a good idea anyway (more on this topic in chaps. 12 and 13). An advantage of working with a small house is that they are more likely to keep your book in print longer. I have also found them to be more accessible and easy to work with.

Within the category of small publishers are university presses. These publishers tend to publish a small number of titles each year. Often, they have a particular niche in which they tend to publish, such as on a certain topic and/or within a specific geographical region (e.g., New England), and they don't typically publish books for the general reader—that is, in a conversational tone. They also tend to be more prestigious than other small presses, at least in academic circles (Niles, 2005).

Large Publishers

Through a series of mergers and acquisitions, as of this writing, the publishing world now has only six major houses. Each of these houses has a number of imprints under their auspices. They are as follows (Niles, 2005):

- Pearson: includes Penguin, Putnam, Viking, Dutton, and others.

- Bertelsmann: includes Random House, Knopf, Anchor, Bantam, Doubleday, Vintage, and Crown.
- TimeWarner: includes Warner Books; Time, Inc.; and others.
- Holtzbrinck: includes St. Martin's Press; Macmillan; Farrar, Straus & Giroux; and others.
- Murdoch's News Corps: includes 20th Century Fox, Fox, HarperCollins, Viacom, Simon & Schuster, Pocket Books, and others.

The advantages of publishing with a large house are that they usually have bigger budgets to promote your book. They can offer larger advances. And there is prestige associated with signing with a major publisher. This may make it easier for you to sell another project.

On the other hand, beginning authors may find themselves out in the cold as their publishers' promotion dollars get put toward more established authors. The publisher may also sign a contract with you but then decide not to publish your book if there hasn't been sufficient interest in prepublication sales. A smaller publisher is less likely to do this. If you submit a manuscript to any of the imprints in a conglomerate, they keep a record of it. If your manuscript is rejected by one imprint, another imprint within the same conglomerate is unlikely to pick it up (Niles, 2005). They can also be more bureaucratic and less accessible. And because they are big, they may do whatever they want with your book. Your choice? Take it or leave it. That can be unpleasant.

Self-Publishing

Self-publishing has a long and venerated history in the United States, and it is another fast-growing segment of the publishing world (Klems, 2005b). Some very famous people self-published their work, including Benjamin Franklin; Ernest Hemingway; and, more recently, Deepak Chopra (Niles, 2005). Self-publishing is not the same as using a vanity press. In self-publishing, you invest your own money in your book. And you reap the profits. Rather than receiving 10% of sales as royalties, you receive 40%, 50%, or more for each book you sell. That difference can be considerable. It also gives you a chance to bring a book to market that publishers weren't interested in and ensures that you make all of the major decisions about how it is written, marketed, and priced.

Some authors have also found self-publishing to be helpful when their books have gone out of print with traditional publishers. Authors re-release their books as self-published volumes. Other authors have used self-publishing as a way to break into a market and, if sales are good, to convince traditional publishers to pick up their work.

The downside of self-publishing is that you have to do all of the marketing yourself. Before you dive in, consider whether you are ready to do that. You need to have a well-established platform for selling your work. You also need to consider your temperament and skills in sales. If your sales skills are poor, you may end up with 10,000 copies of your book sitting in your garage. Self-publishing basically means opening a small business. If you are going to succeed in any small business venture, you must have a clear business plan, know your market, and have a way to market your product. This will not happen on a whim. There is money to be made in self-publishing. But only for people who have done their homework.

There is much more to self-publishing than I can describe in this chapter. But if you think this is something you might like to try, I'd encourage you to read *The Complete Guide to Self-Publishing*, by Tom and Marilyn Ross (2002), and Dan Poynter's *Self-Publishing Manual* (2006). Both are excellent and will give you step-by-step advice.

Below are the stories of two academic colleagues who opted for self-publishing. The first story is about an author of two self-published volumes that he wanted to sell to a traditional publisher. The second story is about a self-published author who ended up starting a small press.

Self-Publishing Story I: Mike Mangan, Self-Publisher to Traditional Publisher. Mike Mangan is a psychology professor at the University of New Hampshire. I asked him to describe the books he has written and his reasons for deciding to self-publish. Here is what he said:

> My first effort was self-publication of a "cross-market" book on sexual behavior that occurs during sleep that would appeal to academic professionals and to folks in

general. I've sold a few hundred copies with no real marketing effort. Because of this effort, along with an academic publication, I have emerged as one of the few "experts" on this topic (I just did two live radio interviews last night). I think some topics are too important to target academic journals and traditional publication routes—initially, that is. It takes too long to get the word out. So I guess I'm a maverick of sorts, bucking the system.

I recently self-published another book on surf etiquette. It has sold quite well. I treated it as my "summer job" last summer—going 'round to surf shops. It was fun. That's one reason why I wrote it. Also, I wrote the book because I've been surfing for 25 years. Over this period of time, I've observed crowding and violence increase. There's violence in the water, which goes against the spirit of surfing. I wrote the book for beginning surfers to give them a "heads up." I also wrote it for veterans because they are the ones who are sick and tired of "newbies" who don't know the rules cluttering up the water.

I will seek traditional publishers for both books as both have shown sales potential. I am not the academic type who, nose to the grindstone, can focus on one topic. I like to pursue my interests, which are broad.

Self-Publishing Story II: Thomas Hale and Hale Publishing. Tom Hale is a pharmacologist and professor of pediatrics at Texas Tech University Medical School. He is also the author and publisher of the wildly successful *Medications and Mothers' Milk* (2006). This volume has become the "bible" of lactational pharmacology, giving clinicians accurate and evidence-based information on which drugs breastfeeding women can safely take. Hale first conceived the idea for this book, now in its 12th edition, in 1990 when his department chair asked him to lecture on drugs and breastfeeding. From there, he started to think through how a mother's body metabolized medications and how the characteristics of individual medications influenced the amount that got into her milk:

> In 1992, I produced a list of drugs on floppy disk. A WIC employee asked me to put this information in a book. I produced my first book with 100 pages, and it started to sell. Dramatically. I added more drugs and sold 1,000 copies of the second edition. I contacted several publishers, and they weren't interested. They didn't think there was a market out there, but I knew there was. One publisher was a little bit interested, but they offered me such a small royalty, I knew it would be better if I did it myself.

Tom got to know his market and what they needed to know. He knew that there would be buyers for his book:

> I feel that one of my strengths, as both an author and a speaker, is that I can translate complex information into understandable terms for a wider audience. The book has grown and changed over the years because of input from health care providers. I listened to what they needed and tried to provide it. *Medications and Mothers' Milk* really came from them, not me.

When asked what he would recommend to someone contemplating self-publishing, he had the following advice:

If you are going to self-publish, you have to think of it as a business. You must set up shipping and accounting systems. You also have to figure out who your market is and who will buy your book. If you decide to go with a regular publisher, make sure they have an interest in your topic. Ninety percent of publishers will stop promoting a book after the first year. Go with a publisher who knows the market.

Tom has recently expanded from the role of self-published author to small publisher. His small press, Hale Publishing, releases several titles a year, including a new mother's version of *Medications and Mothers' Milk*.

MAKING A BOOK PITCH

Sometimes opportunities to pitch a book pop up in places where you least expect them. You may be at a conference or meeting, and someone introduces you to an editor. An editor may come to see your presentation. Or an editor may contact you after reading some of your work online. If you've been thinking about writing a book, be ready for these opportunities when they arise. Books often start with you running an idea by an editor. Therefore, if you have a book idea, you need to be ready to describe it in a sentence or two. This is known as *making a pitch*.

I first met the editors from New Harbinger at an American Psychological Association convention. I had been thinking about approaching them with a couple of book ideas, but I didn't have anything in writing at that point. I liked what they did and thought that my books would fit with their line. One of their sales guys saw me pick up their author guidelines at their booth. He told me that their acquisitions editors were having an open meeting that night and strongly encouraged me to go. Truthfully, I wasn't all that thrilled about going. I was tired and wanted to go back to my room to watch some very important TV. But even in my fatigue, I recognized that this was a good opportunity. With little advance warning, I had a chance to pitch a couple of ideas, one of which became the book *The Hidden Feelings of Motherhood* (Kendall-Tackett, 2001). They expressed interest and asked for a proposal. And the rest, as they say, is history.

Life being what it is, however, sometimes you just aren't prepared when these occasions arise. Don't worry! All is not lost. You can still get your foot in the door. First, when you meet an editor, be sure to get their card. You can contact them again when you return to your office and let them know that you enjoyed meeting them. You can follow up later with a letter or an e-mail when you think of a book idea they might like. When you contact them, be sure to mention where you met them or who introduced you to them. Editors meet hundreds of people during their travels and hand out many cards. Unless they spoke with you at length, they are unlikely to remember you with just a name. You can remind them about who you are by mentioning some of the details of where you met.

If you meet with an editor for any length of time, writing a thank-you note is a good idea. It's not absolutely required, but it lets the editor know that you appreciate the time he or she spent with you. And because most people don't do this, the editor is much more likely to remember you. When it's time to evaluate your book proposal, your taking the time to say thank you will have let the editor know that you will probably be nice to work with. And that's always a good thing.

Writers' Conferences

If you have a book idea and are having trouble making contact with editors, consider going to a writers' conference. I had seen ads for writers' conferences for years in magazines. But I had assumed that they were mostly seminars. Little did I know that most conferences also provide opportunities for you to meet with agents and editors. I attended my first writers' conference earlier this year, and it was a revelation. I felt like I had suddenly learned the secret handshake. If you are just starting out, meeting editors at a conference can be a great way to get past the slush pile and get them interested in your work.

At these conferences, you are often given the opportunity to make a limited number of appointments with editors. These appointments are typically 15 minutes long. Be prepared to talk about your book idea concisely. I'd suggest that you pitch no more than two ideas at one of these meetings. Bring some written material, but don't be surprised if they don't want to take it with them. If everyone brought them stuff to read, they'd never get it home. If any editors are interested, offer your materials to them on the spot, but also offer to send the materials later if the editors prefer (and do it promptly).

To make the most of your time, find out ahead of time who will be there. Do your homework and know what kinds of books the editors you want to speak with publish. I had one meeting with an editor from a large house. It happens to be one of my favorite publishers, which I told the editor. He somewhat skeptically asked me why that was so. I mentioned one of my favorite authors who had written several books with them (some of his best). This same author hasn't written a decent book since he went to another house (in my humble opinion). This editor happened to agree. That immediately caught his attention and changed the whole tone of the meeting. Because I knew their publications, the editor was suddenly a lot more interested in what I had to say. He ended by expressing interest in my work and wanted to read a sample chapter and proposal—even though they usually only read materials sent by agents. Moral of the story: Take the time to get to know about any publishers you are interested in working with.

If you are interested in attending a writer's conference, there are many to choose from. A current issue of *Writer's Digest* usually has a listing (that's where I found the one I attended). Your best bet may be one of the larger, more established conferences, because these are likely to attract more editors. But there are conferences to fit all budgets and temperaments. If you know other writers, ask for recommendations. Also check out the conference Web sites to see if the conference is a good match for you. Remember, publishers attend these events hoping to find promising new talent. There's no reason that can't be you!

CONCLUSION

The initial search for a publisher can be pretty intimidating. But remember that publishers want to find talented writers. Be prepared to talk about your project when the opportunity presents itself. Be enthusiastic and accessible. And try to relax. Even if you do a bad job pitching your book on your first (or second or third) attempt, you'll get better with practice. Then one day, you'll meet an editor dying to talk with you about your work. She'll be so impressed that she will ask for a book proposal—the topic of the next chapter.

10

How to Write and Submit a Book Proposal

Thinking like an editor—understanding the kinds of questions that editors ask themselves, consciously or unconsciously, when evaluating an idea can take some of the mystery out of querying . . . if you learn to test your ideas against the same questions an editor asks—before you fire off that submission— you can save yourself headaches and, of course, time.
—David Fryxell (2004, pp. 63–64)

So you have a fabulous idea for a book and have made a successful pitch. Now what? The next step is to put together a proposal to sell your project. Like anything, there is an art to writing a proposal. In this chapter, I share with you the basics of putting one together.

ANATOMY OF A BOOK PROPOSAL

Book proposals are relatively straightforward to write. As you write, think about what the acquisition editor needs from you. They have to try to "sell" your book idea to their marketing team. The more information you can give them about the market for your book, the better. In this section, I'll show you what to do by using text from the actual book proposals I wrote for *Breastfeeding Made Simple* (Mohrbacher & Kendall-Tackett, 2005) and *The Well-Ordered Home* (Kendall-Tackett, 2003).

The first thing to list is your book's *working title*. This is where you give the publisher a tentative title for your work. Be warned that your publisher may change your title. There's actually more to coming up with a book title than might be obvious. Your publisher will base title decisions on an analysis of the market for competing books. They will also consider whether your title is catchy and compels book buyers to pick up your book. The marketing team considers how your title fares in electronic searches on Amazon.com and other online booksellers. Finally, decisions about book titles are based on where your book is likely to be shelved in bookstores.

When I was working on *The Well-Ordered Home*, my editor told me that the marketing team had decided to rename the book *50 Best Ways to Organize Your Home*. I agreed, figuring that they knew better than me what would sell. A couple of months later, I got a call from my editor, who started with, "You're going to laugh." (I did.) It seems that their book distributor had strongly recommended that we go back to the original title. And as you can tell from my earlier references, it ended up being *The Well-Ordered Home*.

The title we originally had for *Breastfeeding Made Simple* was *Secrets of Success*. The publisher suggested the new title, and we liked it. They wanted *breastfeeding* right in the title so it would come up when someone searched under "breastfeeding." They were afraid that "secrets of success" wouldn't be as accessible to electronic searches or as obvious when shelved at a bookstore.

After the title, list *your name and the names of any coauthors* on one line. Your credentials and affiliations will go in another part of the proposal.

In the next section, you provide an *estimate of length*. Always add more pages than you think you will need because most authors have the tendency to go long. I often use a page range. Always specify that you mean manuscript pages (usually double spaced, but always check with the editor), as opposed to typeset pages, which are usually a smaller number. You might propose a manuscript of 250 to 300 pages, for example. Some authors prefer to use word count to estimate pages, which I find a bit odd, but I have seen it done on proposals. So given an average of 250 words per page, take your page count and multiply. For example, a 200-page manuscript would be roughly 50,000 words.

Estimated length is important because length is one factor that determines price. Your publisher will find it easier to sell a book with 200 typeset pages than 500 typeset pages, because longer books cost more to produce and are priced higher. Publishers also make determinations based on the prices of competing works. Your book should be in the same page range if you are going to be competitive with similar titles.

What is your book about? In this section of the proposal, you provide a paragraph-long *book description*. Try to make it catchy and interesting. If it is dull, chances are the editor will not keep reading. The following is the book description for *The Well-Ordered Home*:

> *The Well-Ordered Home* tells readers how to save time, money, and enhance the quality of their lives. Rather than being a compilation of household tips, it presents seven principles that can help readers improve the organization and "flow" of their home.

Next, provide detailed information on who you expect will read your book, or your *intended audience*. The more specific you can be, the better. Writing something like "everyone" lets the publisher know that you really have no idea who your audience is. Who would benefit from your book? Are they old or young? Rich, middle class, or low income? Are they White, Black, Latino, Asian, or Native American? Are they male or female? Are they parents? If so, how old are their children? Are they in any professional organizations, clubs, or support groups? Are they people who frequent certain Web sites or online communities? Are they people from a certain part of the country?

Does your target audience have a specific condition, problem, or disease? If so, say how many people in the United States or other countries have that condition. For example, how many families in the United States have a child with autism? How many people have bipolar disorder, chronic pain, or posttraumatic stress disorder? Books about problems that affect at least a million people have a better chance of being published.

An ancillary question is, how will people find out about your book? The more specific you can be, the more likely your publisher will be to take a chance on publishing your book. With more than 50,000 books published each year, it's more difficult than ever for new authors to get shelf space at bookstores. Many books only sell a few hundred copies, and sometimes the publishers don't even recoup their costs of bringing the book to market. For a few worthy projects, publishers will often proceed anyway. But they can't do that on too many projects and hope to stay in business. Do your homework, and think about how you will get your book noticed.

When describing your target audience, mention any connections you have that will help to sell your book. This is known as your *platform*. Are you in a position of influence for an organization that addresses the topic of your book? Do you have a well-established Web site where people can visit for information? Do you speak at conferences or workshops? Are they organized around the topic of your book? Conferences and workshops are often great places to sell books. Let people know that you will sign their copies. That can often be an added incentive for people to buy from you. One author told me that he often sells books to 40% of his conference audience—a very high percentage—because they want him to sign their copies.

Finally, do you write for publications that go to your target audience? Do you have an established name in the field in which you are writing? This is where writing for magazines and newsletters can make a big difference in book sales. People are more likely to buy if they "know" you and have read (and presumably liked) your previous work.

Now, let's take a look "behind the scenes." When acquisitions editors receive your proposal, presuming they like it, their next stop is the marketing department or, at some houses, one of the directors or the publisher. When they meet with marketing, they will pitch the books that they think have promise; in other words, they'll do a presentation about your book idea. Marketing, being marketing, will ask very specific questions about whether there are enough people interested in the topic to buy the book. They will want to know how to sell this book, what connections the author already has, and what the author is willing to do to promote the book. Make the acquisition editors' job easier by providing the answers for them. If they are interested, the editor may get back to you for further information if you haven't provided enough. But don't count on that. With some publishers, you will only get one bite at the apple. So it's in your best interest to be as thorough as possible right from the start.

With *Breastfeeding Made Simple*, we were able to make a persuasive case for our book. My coauthor and I have spoken at breastfeeding conferences all over the country. And we've rarely spoken at the same conference, so our coverage of the United States, Canada, and even Australia is good. Further, we each have a reputation as experts in our field and knew we could get endorsements from others. Finally, we both had connections with major organizations associated with breastfeeding, which gave us both credibility and access to contacts. It was quite easy for us to line up endorsements from leaders in the field, and we did.

What you need to provide for the editor is proof that (a) there is a market for your book and (b) that you have access to that market and will work hard to sell your book. Author participation in book promotion is a key reason why books succeed. Show the editor that you are willing to do that. Editors are going to be more impressed if you are realistic about the influence you will be able to muster to help to promote your book. Try not to promise something you can't deliver—such as an appearance on Oprah.

Bottom line: Know the market and describe why your project is unique and makes a contribution to the field.

Another crucial part of your book proposal is noting competing works (known as *comps*), and it's essential that you do your homework. Fortunately, online booksellers, such as Amazon.com, make this easier than ever.

Find out what's already out there on your topic and read those books. Then list the books that are most similar to the one you are proposing. Tell the editor about the focus of each book, when it was published, who the audience is, and how well it is selling. After describing each book, discuss how it compares with the book you are proposing. Will your book have a different slant or theoretical framework? Is the competing book out of date? Is it too technical or not technical enough? Is it written for a different audience than you plan to reach? What will your book add to the existing knowledge base? Does it have any unusual features?

Your editor may ask you for the Amazon.com ranking for each title; the smaller the number, the better (see chap. 13). Your publisher wants to know how similar books are selling. If the numbers are too high (e.g., over 300,000), then that may indicate that books on this particular topic don't sell well. On the other hand, if you can find comps with numbers under 10,000, the publisher may be more interested, because it means that people are buying books on that topic. Publishers are often reluctant, especially with trade books, to be the first to publish a book on a topic—unless it's exceptional. In contrast, academic publishers are more comfortable with being first.

Also consider whether there are too many competing titles. Publishers are often reluctant to take on a project when the field is already saturated. But this is not always a problem. For some topics, such as home organization, people will buy multiple titles on the same topic.

It is interesting to note that the marketing department at New Harbinger originally turned down our idea for a breastfeeding book. There were several reasons for this. First, they felt the market was already saturated, meaning that there were too many competing works already on the market. Second, they had no other titles on this topic, so they were worried about how they would market it. And third, they couldn't see how our book would be unique. Fortunately, the editor shared these concerns with me, and I was able to address them.

With regard to market saturation, I pointed out that one of the books the publisher cited as competition for ours was written by my coauthor. It was a book for professionals, and it had a decent Amazon.com rank (around 24,000). The other books they cited were all several years old and were using information that had become outdated. In recent years, there had been several major breakthroughs in the understanding of breastfeeding. Those of us in field now recognized that much of the information used in the major texts and in books for mothers had been disproven by current research. These changes had huge ramifications for how we counseled mothers. My coauthor's previous book for professionals, *The Breastfeeding Answer Book* (Mohrbacher & Stock, 2003), was the first text that incorporated this new research. No books written for mothers before then had included this information.

In our proposal, we included a discussion of how our book differed from others on the market. This discussion involved naming the competition and explaining in detail why we thought our book would sell. We included the following three paragraphs, and you could do something similar for the topic of your book.

By and large, breastfeeding books sell well. Two of the most well-known are La Leche League International's *The Womanly Art of Breastfeeding* and Kathleen Huggins's *Nursing Mothers' Companion*. Both of these books are excellent, and offer mothers much valuable information.

While these books are good, there is room for one more. Our book offers three distinct differences.

1. The U.S. Department of Health and Human Services is launching an important advertising campaign in support of breastfeeding in 2004. These public service announcements are produced by the Ad Council, and are based on extensive research. In these advertisements, they consider breastfeeding the norm, and all other approaches as sub-optimum. Rather than emphasize the benefits of breastfeeding (the approach taken by all the other books on the market), they will emphasize the risks of not breastfeeding. While this might seem a subtle shift in language, there are major implications. Our book will be the first to use the new language.

2. The field of human lactation has recently undergone some major changes. Breastfeeding has been studied and conceptualized in a completely different way. Fundamental assumptions have been called into question. One example of this change has to do with

the structure of the lactating breast. Recent research using ultrasound has demonstrated that even physical structures that have appeared on breast anatomy diagrams for 150 years, such as milk sinuses, do not exist. Until recently, milk sinuses were considered the anatomical basis for many clinical practices, such as techniques for manual expression of milk and latch-on. Most current books reflect the old information. This current information is so new that it has not trickled down to a general audience. Our book will be the first to integrate this material in a book for mothers.

3. Our book will be organized around seven laws that are unique to this book. These laws summarize and incorporate the latest research on breastfeeding. They are easy for mothers to understand, and can help mothers avoid some of the pitfalls they often face.

There is no need to trash the books you compare yours with. In fact, it's probably better if you don't, because your publisher may ask the authors of these books to review your proposal as an expert in that field. But you can point out strengths and limitations of that work and how your proposed work will extend the knowledge base in some important ways. Once we made all of these connections for the editor, she was able to go back to her marketing group and get them to accept our proposal.

Author qualifications is where you get to explain why you are qualified—indeed, the best person—to write the book. You don't want to just recite your curriculum vitae here, however. What you want to do is summarize, in two to three paragraphs, what your qualifications are for this particular project. Keep in mind what the editor needs from you and what they might be nervous about. Remember, your editor will need to persuade marketing that you are the one to write this book. So try to anticipate the questions that marketing might raise and address them.

You need to establish why you are expert on this topic. What types of life experiences have you had that are relevant to the book you are proposing? What are your professional credentials? How many years of experience do you have? Have you been volunteering for related organizations? Do you have any other types of credentials that are relevant?

Prior publications, on this or on related topics, are important to mention because they help to establish you as an expert. Even if your publications are on another topic, they tell the editor that you have a history of getting work done. This is important, because your editor has most likely had the experience of someone promising them work and sounding good on paper but failing to deliver the goods. Below is a summary of my coauthor's qualifications from our proposal:

> Nancy is an International Board Certified Lactation Consultant. She has been an accredited La Leche League leader for more than 20 years, and was president of a highly successful Chicago-area lactation private practice for 10 years. The material presented in *Secrets*

of Success came from Nancy's hands-on work with thousands of mothers. Her current position is Lactation Education Specialist, at Hollister, a medical supply company and maker of the Ameda breast pumps. She is their lactation expert and travels extensively to provide training to lactation professionals all over the country.

Nancy has recently completed the third edition of her best-selling *The Breastfeeding Answer Book*. The previous two editions of this book sold more than 100,000 copies worldwide, and have been translated into four languages. Because of this work, she has contact with lactation researchers from all over the world. Many of these researchers generously shared even pre-published studies with her. She has access to cutting-edge research, and is used to writing for both professional and lay audiences. Nancy wrote the breastfeeding column for *Baby Talk* magazine for five years, was the editor of *New Beginnings*, the La Leche League magazine for mothers, and has written a number of articles and monographs for mothers about breastfeeding.

The next part of your proposal is a detailed outline of your book. Generally, I title each chapter, then write a paragraph or two for each. Below I've included the description of the introduction and first two chapters.

Section I: The Seven Natural Laws of Breastfeeding
The format of the next seven chapters will be the same. We will describe the natural law, how it works, and how mothers can use it to help them breastfeed. Then we will describe some of the factors that interfere with that law. Finally, we'll describe what mothers can do to get back to basics, and make the law work for them— even when they've gotten off to a bad start.

Chapter 1: Babies Have the Urge to Self-Attach

Babies are born "hard-wired" to breastfeed. If not inter-fered with, healthy babies will crawl to the breast, latch themselves on, and begin breastfeeding. Unfortunately, in many cases, hospital routines prevent these natural reflexes from being triggered. Mothers who know about these reflexes can use them to get breastfeeding off to a good start. Even when mothers have difficulties at the beginning, these reflexes can be used to solve prob-lems by giving babies the opportunity to do what they were born to do.

Chapter 2: Use the Power of Skin-to-Skin: A Baby's Natural Habitat

Before birth, babies are inside their mothers' bodies. They smell her, feel her and hear her every moment of their day. Once they are born, most babies are routinely whisked away from their mothers. This is the normal order of things, experts assure us. But we are now learn-ing that the "experts" were wrong. Being away from mothers is physically stressful for babies, and now we have the scientific data to prove it. In some situations and in some parts of the world, the power of skin-to-skin has made the difference between life and death. The power of skin-to-skin is one of the newly under-stood laws of breastfeeding that can prevent or alleviate the stress of separation and solve many breastfeeding problems.

After reviewing your outline, an interested pub-lisher may also ask you for a *sample chapter* or two. Before you start to write, ask the acquisitions editor with whom you are working if he or she has a preference for a particular chapter. If your editor has no preference, then write the chapters that are easiest for you to write.

Personally, I find writing sample chapters to be very difficult. However, publishers tend to want these from authors for several reasons: to check your writing style, to see if you can complete work to deadline, and to see how closely you adhere to your outline. One publisher told me that when they have not asked for sample chapters from authors, they've been sorry. Either the author never gets around to writing the book, or the author, often an academic, writes so technically or so poorly that it takes major amounts of editing to have a workable draft.

I've had to write sample chapters for about half of the books I've sold. Something interesting I've observed is that once I get a contract, I usually take the sample chapter I wrote and scatter it across several chapters as I write the actual book. That's even true of this book. The sample chapter I wrote is now part of the introduction and chapters 3 and 4.

The final component to a book proposal is your *cover letter and curriculum vitae* (CV). The cover letter in an electronic submission is generally just the e-mail you send with attachments. You could also write a more formal cover letter on your electronic stationery. I made myself some letterhead using MS Word that includes my name, work address, affiliation, phone and fax numbers, and e-mail and Web site addresses. Make it easy for people to find you.

Also attach a copy of your CV. Make sure that it is current and neatly typed. Having received a lot of CVs over the years, I can tell you that a surprising number are poorly laid out. Although I don't think it's necessary to have a slickly produced CV, do try to make it easy to read. Finally, thank the editor or publisher for their time and let them know that you are happy to provide any additional information that they would like.

Conclusion

Writing a book proposal is an important first step in writing a book. If you are someone who likes to have a contract ahead of time, it's important for you to do this task well. Fortunately, book proposals are relatively easy to write and will help you think through—perhaps for the first time—the focus and slant of the book you want to write.

11

Sign on the Dotted Line:
An Overview of Book Contracts

The publishing agreement is the single most important
document in a book deal, the Bible and the Constitution
of the business dealings between author and publisher,
the place where rights and duties (and money!) are allocated.
. . . And so, although there's always a temptation . . .
to "just sign it," the book publishing contract ought to be
vigorously negotiated, carefully drafted, and meticulously
scrutinized by both parties before it is signed.
—Jonathan Kirsch (1995, p. 59)

If you decide to work with a traditional publisher,
another step in your journey is negotiating a book
contract. In this chapter, I review the basics of book
contracts. Even if you are just starting out, it's good
to know your way around a contract. If you have concerns, it's better to ask your questions now, before you
sign. If you're still not sure, ask an attorney. This
chapter is not a substitute for legal advice.

Things to Keep in Mind

Keep a couple of things in mind when negotiating a publishing contract. First, publishers are in business to make money. Because of that, they will negotiate the best deal for themselves. Most of them are not trying to cheat you. But neither are they a social service agency, looking out for your good above their own (Fishman, 2004a).

Second, publishers have room to negotiate, to a greater or lesser extent (Fishman, 2004a). As with anything, you'll be able to get a better deal if you have more leverage (e.g., more experience and/or a hot topic). If you're just starting out, you may not be able to make many changes to a contract you are offered. This may also be true if you are working with a larger publisher whose contracts are often boilerplate and can't be changed. But it doesn't hurt to ask. If there is something you don't like, ask your editor if he or she can modify the agreement (Feiertag & Cupito, 2004). Parts of your contract can be amended or deleted altogether.

In this chapter, I cover three main sections of a book contract: the transfer of copyright, author compensation, and delivery of the manuscript. These are described below. The focus of this chapter is book contracts. Given the amount of work involved in writing a book, you have the most to lose if you don't understand what you are doing. But contracts for magazine articles usually have similar clauses and typically involve the transfer of copyright for first serial rights (or "first serial North American rights"), international rights, and electronic rights; delivery of the manuscript; and terms of payment. In my experience, these contracts are generally shorter and less complicated than their book counterparts. For more information about publishing magazine articles, see chapter 8.

COPYRIGHT 101

One of the primary purposes of a book contract is to specify the terms of transfer or assignment of your copyright to the publisher. In this section, I provide a basic overview of copyright law. As a writer, it's good for you to understand the different rights that you have as an author so that you do not inadvertently sign away more than you intend.

Copyright Notice

Copyright is a legal tool that gives the author of a work control over how it can be used by others. Most works of authorship (writing, music, plays, photographs, etc.) are entitled to protection as long as they fulfill three basic requirements: fixation, originality, and minimal creativity. *Fixation* means that the work has been fixed "in a tangible means of expression"; in other words, it can be accessed in some medium such as paper, a computer file, a recording, or a canvas. *Originality* refers to the work being new in some appreciable degree, although not necessarily completely novel. For example, in a version of a work derived from others (e.g., a screenplay version of a classic novel), the new element can be copyright protected, because some original components have been added even though the work is derivative. Minimal creativity implies at least some degree of novelty (Fishman, 2004b).

Copyrights have an interesting history in the United States. They were actually considered so important to the Founding Fathers that they were stipulated even before the First Amendment was drafted. Copyright protection was provided to "promote the progress of science and useful arts, by securing, for limited times to authors and inventors, the exclusive right to their respective writings and discoveries" (Article I, Section 8, Clause 8 of the original U.S. Constitution, quoted in Wilson, 2003, p. 3). The idea was to give people a financial incentive for creativity by letting them profit from their ideas. Eventually, copyright expires and these works become part of the "public domain," available to everyone. That way, the law served both the needs of the individual and the wider society. (For more information about the basics of copyright, copyright terms, and the public domain, visit the U.S. Copyright Office Web site: http://www.copyright.gov.)

With any material you produce, it's a good idea for you to post a copyright notice. Although not strictly necessary, because anything you produce is immediately protected, having a clearly posted copyright notice can be helpful if you ever take legal action against someone for infringing on your copyright (Fishman, 2004a; Wilson, 2003; Zaharoff, 2005).

A copyright notice has three elements (Fishman, 2004a). The first is the word *copyright* or the symbol "©." Many authors use both. The second element is the year of first publication. This is followed by the third element, the name of the copyright holder. When writing your name as copyright holder, it's best if you use your full legal name rather than a nickname. So, a complete copyright notice for me would be as follows:

Copyright © 2006 by Kathleen A. Kendall-Tackett.

Some copyright experts recommend that you also follow up with the statement, "All rights reserved." With this, you have given notice to any reader that the material they are reading is copyrighted, and someone infringing on your copyright can't claim that they didn't know (Wilson, 2003; Zaharoff, 2005).

Registration of Copyright

Registration of copyright isn't strictly necessary because copyright is automatic. But it gives you greater legal protection if your copyright is infringed on. If your copyright is violated and the work was registered ahead of time, you can even collect attorney's fees. Registering a copyright is simple. You submit an application to the copyright office, pay a fee of $45, and submit one copy of your work (Zaharoff, 2005).

Copyright in Publishing Agreements

Your copyright actually includes many rights, including the right to reproduce and distribute the work, to create derivative works, to display or perform the work, and to license or sell audio or visual rights to the work. When you sign a book contract, you transfer some or all of these rights to your publisher (Zaharoff, 2005). Copyright can be divided and licensed any number of ways, including by language, type of media (e.g., hard cover, soft cover, electronic), time, or geography (e.g., U.S. Rights, North American Rights, or World Rights; Fishman, 2004a).

Types of Rights

Publishing rights are not a monolithic entity; there is an entire range of rights available to you as the author. Rather than think about rights as a unit, author and intellectual property attorney Jonathan Kirsch (1995) recommended that you think about copyright as a bundle of individual rights. Before you sign any agreement, make sure that you know which rights you are assigning to the publisher.

All Rights (or All World Rights)

When you assign all rights, it means that the publisher owns the rights to any print versions of your writing, any electronic rights, and any subsidiary rights, which include other products made from your writing (see below). In other words, the publisher becomes the sole owner of your work (Fishman, 2004a).

If your contract specifies that you assign world rights to the publisher, ask your acquisitions editor for more information. Under what terms would your publisher bring the book out as an audiobook or an e-book? How would you be compensated for these versions? Will the book be sold and promoted around the world? What kind of collaboration has your publisher established with international publishers for licensing translations? If your publisher has a good track record for handling some of these subsidiary rights (e.g., finding the best publisher for bringing out the book in paper), you may wish to retain this clause, with language added in the subsidiary rights section clarifying how you will be compensated for each version of your work.

Subsidiary Rights

Subsidiary rights are rights the publisher acquires for potential release of your work in other formats. Some common kinds of rights are translations, paperback rights, electronic rights, audio rights, and dramatic (movie) rights. The publisher may itself publish your work in any of these formats or may sell or license any of those rights to other houses. If you believe your book has high potential for sale as an audio book or in paperback format, for example, discuss those prospects with your acquisition editor and request concrete language that specifies how the creation of such versions would be handled and how you would be compensated. You should also ask that clear language be included specifying under what terms any of these rights revert to you.

Electronic Rights

With the ascendancy of the Internet, authors and publishers frequently negotiate over electronic rights. Electronic rights include all versions of your work in electronic media, CD-ROM, online magazines, and even interactive games (Feiertag & Cupito, 2004). In the world of easy iPod downloads, readers are growing accustomed to accessing all kinds of information in electronic format. Review the electronic rights clause in your contract carefully and ask that language be included that details how you will be compensated for the sale, licensing, or publication of your work in electronic format. If you assign these rights to your publisher, you may even be forbidden to post your materials on your own Web site. I had one book from which I had posted sample chapters on my Web site. My editor (nicely) let me know that I was in violation of my copyright agreement. She told me to take those chapters down and checked a few days later to see that I had.

Kirsch (1995) also recommended that you not sign away your rights to "future media" (i.e., media that are not invented yet), because this could also be an important source of future revenue. If electronic rights are not specified in an agreement, the presumption is that they stay with you (Feiertag & Cupito, 2004), but it would be wise to request that this be spelled out.

Within the category of electronic rights, there are several subcategories, which I describe below (Feiertag & Cupito, 2004).

First Electronic Rights. Assigning your publisher first electronic rights gives them the opportunity to publish the electronic version first. You retain the right to publish your material later. A variant is "First World-wide Electronic Rights," because the Internet goes beyond any national borders.

Be aware that if you have published something on the Web, whether via a blog or Web site, you cannot sell the first electronic rights. The law considers you to have already published this material. However, if you inform the editor you are working with that the material has already been posted on the Web, you may be able to work something out (Klems, 2005a).

Nonexclusive Electronic Rights. With this type of agreement, you are free to resell your material indefinitely. The downside is that the publisher can also resell your material without compensating you further (Feiertag & Cupito, 2004).

Exclusive Electronic Rights. With this type of agreement, the publisher has sole claim on your material. Feiertag and Cupito (2004) suggested that you only sign this type of agreement for a limited amount of time (e.g., 6 months), after which you are free to resell your work. You might opt for a longer time frame if the level of compensation warrants it. Once these rights revert to you, you are free to resell your material as long as you indicate that it has been previously published elsewhere.

Archival Rights. Your publisher may want to have your article or other material available indefinitely in online archives. If you agree to this, try to have the agreement be nonexclusive so you can resell or reuse these articles (Feiertag & Cupito, 2004).

Reversion of Rights and Remainders

Be sure there is language in the contract spelling out when the rights revert to you. Typically, this happens when your book goes out of print. But with the increasing popularity of electronic publishing, that may technically never happen. If the rights revert back to you, this should be specified in your contract (Feiertag & Cupito, 2004). Ideally, when your book goes out of print, your publisher will send a letter informing you that your book is slated to go out of print by a certain date. When your book is officially out of print, you'll get another letter assigning the copyright back to you.

When your book is going out of print, you will usually be offered the *remainders*, or books still in stock. These are usually available for a low price (e.g., $2.00 a copy). I'd encourage you to buy these if you can. You'll want to keep a few copies. And you can sell the rest.

I've had two books go out of print. Both times, I bought all the remainders and was able to find good homes for them. Most recently, I bought the remaining 200 or so copies of the first edition of *The Hidden Feelings of Motherhood* (Kendall-Tackett, 2001). I went to the page for that book on Amazon.com, indicated that I wanted to sell my copies, listed them for $2.00 off the list price, made a note that books were "signed by the author," and sold them all.

I also asked my publisher to send me the electronic files for that book, which had all the edits we had worked so hard to make. These files made my job a lot easier when I wrote a second edition for another publisher. Speaking of which, I used some of my re-mainder copies to find a new publisher. The second edition was released less than a year after the book officially went out of print.

Work for Hire

Another type of publishing agreement is *work for hire*. Under this type of agreement, you write something for a fee. The law does not recognize you as the author of the work; the person who paid for it is (Zaharoff, 2005). Generally speaking, you must sign an explicit work-for-hire agreement. If you do, you do not own the writing you produce. That means you have no right to sell it, prepare a variant work based on it, or even read it in public without permission (Fishman, 2004a).

A colleague of mine had once signed a work-for-hire agreement with a granting body. As part of that grant, she developed an assessment tool and had made a bunch of copies she wanted to sell at a conference I was chairing. I had to tell her that she couldn't sell them there because she did not own the copyright to that material. She protested that the assessment tool was her "intellectual property," completely oblivious to the fact that she had signed her rights to this material away. Word to the wise: Know what you are signing.

The writing you do as part of your job can also be considered work for hire. Fortunately, academic publications are usually exempt from this rule because their content is not specified by the employer. Rather, professors are encouraged to publish (or perish), but what they write is up to them (Fishman, 2004a). Agreeing to write a work for hire is obviously the least advantageous for you. Even so, there may be circumstances under which it makes sense for you to enter into this type of agreement. I've written one work for hire. I was hired to write a training manual for a branch of the military. I wasn't interested in using that work for anything else. So the work-for-hire arrangement was fine with me. (And to be perfectly frank, the money was good.)

If you do agree to write a work for hire, Fishman (2004a) also recommended that you stipulate in your agreement that your name be included on it if that is important to you. Works for hire become the property of the person who purchased them. They don't have to even list your name unless you have it in your agreement.

COMPENSATION

Although money is only one of several reasons to write a book, you don't want to be silly or naive about the financial end. Even if you don't make a lot of money (and most publications won't), you'll want to receive at least some compensation for all of your hard work. Compensation can take several forms, including royalties, advances, author discounts, and author copies. These forms are described below.

Royalties

Your contract will specify the amount of royalties that you can expect. This is usually listed as a percentage rather than a flat rate per book sold. This figure will be based on either the net price (what the publisher receives) or the list price of each book. If the figure is based on the net price, that means less money for you. For large retailers, such as Amazon.com, publishers have to offer a deep discount, so their net is less. But they will likely sell a lot more books.

The percentage that you receive can vary widely. A 10% royalty is fairly typical, especially for a first-time author. But you may see percentages as low as 5% or as high as 15%. When you are offered a low rate, it may be on the first 1,000 copies sold, with increases after that. Academic books often have a higher percentage, but you sell fewer of them.

You may also be able to negotiate the percentage you receive for royalties. Your publisher may be able to give you an extra percentage point or two. It doesn't hurt to ask. Your contract will also stipulate how often you will get royalty statements and payments. These can vary from once a year to once a quarter. It's helpful to keep track of that date. I hadn't heard from one publisher in 15 months. I checked my contract, and then got in touch with my editor. Sure enough, they "hadn't known" where to send the statements and checks. They sent them to me soon thereafter.

Advances Against Royalties

Something else that's specified in your contract is *advances you receive against royalties*. As the term implies, this is money you receive up front that will be charged against any money you earn from royalties. This payment is often divided into two or three payments. You'll generally receive the first payment on signing an agreement; the second when the completed manuscript is turned in; and, in some cases, a third payment when the manuscript is published (Kirsch, 1995).

Thanks to news reports of celebrities receiving six-figure advances, authors often have a very inflated idea of how much they are going to get for an advance. I hate to break this to you, but you probably aren't going to get a huge advance (if any) as a first-time author. According to Tom Connor (2006), a typical advance for a first-time author is $2,500 to $15,000. Even as an experienced author, if a small or academic press is publishing your book, you may not get much of an advance. Some give none.

Honestly, this suits me just fine, but I realize I'm fairly unusual in this regard. I abhor debt. And an advance against future earning feels like just that. That being said, I realize that lots of other authors feel differently and look at an advance as a measure of esteem that the publisher has for them. Also, as publicist Lissa Warren (2004) pointed out, if a publisher has given you a large advance, they're likely to invest more in promoting your book. She has a solid point.

The editor that you're working with often has some discretion about offering an advance as well. So if you want an advance, definitely say something. Just don't expect that a small press will be able to furnish one. They probably can't afford to pay out a lot of money before they get manuscripts. It doesn't mean that they don't think highly of you. It's just not smart for them to do business that way.

Author Discounts

Something I consider more important than percentage of royalties is the author discount. If you don't ever have occasion to sell your books directly, this may be less important to you. However, it's worth asking about. What this refers to is the discount at which you can buy your books. Forty percent is fairly typical, but three of the publishers I work with give me a 50% discount. That's even better.

In addition to your discount, be sure to note whether there is a prohibition against you reselling your book. If there is, I would fight to remove that clause. As I described earlier, selling books yourself, usually in conjunction with seminars or workshops that you teach, can be a substantial source of revenue—many times the royalties you receive. So if you speak at conferences at all, make sure that you are allowed to resell your book.

Author Copies

The number of free copies that you are entitled to is also stipulated in your contract. A typical arrangement is 10 copies. But you may be able to get more. If you are editing a book, be sure to find out about contributor copies. The first book I edited did not provide contributor copies to all of the coauthors of my chapters—only to the first author. Frankly, I didn't know enough to ask. But now I do!

You can also ask for a certain number of review copies in addition to your author copies. These are the copies you send out to journals or books for review or send to interested journalists. Your publisher is usually also willing to send these copies out, but sometimes it's nice to have a few on hand for those last-minute opportunities that arise.

I give my author copies to people who invite me to speak at their conferences; to the media; to people who are writing reviews for Amazon.com or other sites; to key people in the field; and of course, to my mom and dad. The more author copies you can get, the better (and cheaper) it will be for you.

DELIVERY OF THE MANUSCRIPT
AND OTHER CONTRACT ISSUES

In addition to copyright and compensation, there are some other issues that are part of most book contracts. I've included a brief summary of these below. Be aware that you can often negotiate about these as well. But keep in mind that you won't always get what you ask for. Be willing to compromise, and focus on the aspects you find most important.

Manuscript Format

Your contract will spell out the particulars of the manuscript you need to deliver to your publisher. This will include the date it's due, the number of pages of the total manuscript, and the format in which the publisher would like to receive it. Be aware that if you do not do as your contract specifies, the publisher can terminate your agreement. They probably won't, but know that they legally could.

The publisher could also reject your manuscript if they are not happy with the finished product or you failed to deliver what you promised (Kirsch, 1995). Two things can help protect you from this. The first is a developmental edit, in which the publisher sees your work in its formative stages (see chap. 7). The second is a detailed book proposal (see chap. 10). As I mentioned earlier, books often evolve in unexpected ways. That's normal. But if you find that your manuscript is moving in a direction that substantially differs from the contracted volume, don't wait to "surprise" your editor with this news. Communicate with your editor early rather than later. I've found that most of my editors were amenable to changes—even big ones. But I kept them in the loop.

Your publisher also has the option of terminating your agreement for nondelivery of the manuscript. Some publishers are remarkably tolerant of flaky academic authors. You'll likely find this less true with trade publishers. As I mentioned before, don't expect your editor to just wink at your naughty behavior. Publishing is a business, not day care. If you are late, especially if you haven't communicated with your editor, your publisher has the right to revoke your contract. And if you were paid an advance, you may have to cough that back up as well (Feiertag & Cupito, 2004).

Proofs and Indexing

Something else that is often stipulated in a contract is the review of proofs. Find out if you will have the right to review the final version of your edited manuscript before it goes to the printer (Feiertag & Cupito, 2004). As I described in chapter 7, some publishers will let you make substantive edits to galleys. Others will not. Your contract may also stipulate when you need to return your proofs (e.g., within 14 days). If the publisher doesn't hear from you and doesn't get marked galleys from you, they have the right to proceed to publication without your final review. Publishers will generally contact you before sending you proofs to find out if you are available during that time.

You may also have some room to negotiate here. On two different occasions, I've had publishers ask whether they could send me proofs right when I was traveling a lot or had another pressing deadline. In both cases, I was able to move the deadline back a couple of weeks. But once again, communication is key. Call your editor and work out a deal.

Something else to find out is who will pay for indexing your book (Feiertag & Cupito, 2004). *Indexing* refers to the process of going through the book and creating a subject and sometimes an author index. I'm embarrassed to admit that I've been surprised by this a couple of times. I've gotten a substantially smaller royalty check because indexing was deducted. Are you expected to index the book? Or will the publisher? What will be the charge for indexing? You may find that it is worth it to have the publisher do it, even for a fee. But know ahead of time, and make a conscious decision.

Cover, Back Material, and Title

Consider stipulating in your contract final approval of the cover, back material, and title. Cover, back material, and title are part of your publisher's efforts to market your book. Your publisher may make decisions on these based on how your book will be placed. Often, it's in your best interests to cede to these decisions. But it's appropriate for you to be in on the decisions.

I want to warn you that even if final approval is stipulated, you may not get it. Sometimes the person making the promise (often the acquisitions editor) doesn't have control over the production team. She may promise final approval in good faith, but what you actually experience can be quite different.

I remember one time being sent a cover for my "approval." In the cover e-mail, I was immediately told that I couldn't change the cover art or make any other changes. That was too bad. I thought the cover was ugly and looked like blood. I frankly wondered why we even bothered with the "approval" step, because I hadn't been allowed to change a thing. Fortunately, I've been happy with all of the rest of my covers.

Approval of back material is something I always stipulate in my contract. *Back material* is the paragraph description of your book on the front flap of the dust jacket or on the back cover. It may be the only thing a potential book buyer reads and therefore needs to be accurate. Unfortunately, I've had two occasions on which back material on my books was actually wrong. The copywriter used material from the original proposal, not the finished product. Not good!

Finally, I'd ask for final approval on the title. Sometimes, publishers will change titles, often with good reason. Several of my books have ended up with different titles, and I'm generally fine with the changes. But I want to be able to approve them. I've had at least two friends whose publishers changed their titles at the last minute. They've both been unhappy with the result.

Title, back material, and cover are ultimately business decisions that your publisher will make on the basis of their experience with the market. The final decision is theirs. But it's in their best interest and yours to make sure the information is factually correct. If you let your publisher know that that's what you are concerned about, you may find they are amenable to involving you in this process.

Competing Works

One other contract clause bears mentioning here, and that is the clause against publishing competing works. The competing-works clause is to keep you from publishing something that will directly compete with the book you are proposing. Sometimes people worry that this means that you aren't able to publish anything on the same topic. Don't worry! That's not the case. But as Feiertag and Cupito (2004) recommended, make sure that what constitutes a competing work is narrowly defined. You don't want the definition to be so broad that it could include any of your future work on a topic.

I've had noncompete clauses with two of my books. In both cases, they were easily addressed. First, I contacted each of my editors before I signed the contract and told them I had a similar book under consideration.

I had to write a letter to each stipulating why these books were different from each other. Once the editors received these letters, my publishers modified the non-compete clauses, and I was able to work on both projects without further incident.

CONCLUSION

Depending on your previous work, you may have had little experience with selecting a publisher or negotiating contracts. But it is in your best interest to have at least some knowledge about the business end of publications. So ask questions and realize that you can bargain with your publisher. If in doubt, seek legal advice. Negotiating carefully at the beginning will help you have a more positive publishing experience rather than one you will regret.

12

Book Promotion I: Working With a Publicist and the Media

Without a doubt, as an author you need to know how to navigate the waters of book PR, not just to maintain your sanity and calm your nerves, but because you're your book's most important asset.
—Lissa Warren (2004, p. xiv)

You've turned your book in. Now, all you need to do is sit back and wait for the royalty checks to start rolling in. Right? Wrong! The next phase of the process is as important as writing: You need to promote your work. The hard truth is that most publishers don't have the resources to do beyond the minimum amount of promotion for beginning authors. But does that mean that you are helpless? Absolutely not!

I remember with my first book being upset about the lack of promotion. It wasn't until I read Judith Appelbaum's (1998) classic, *How to Get Happily Published*, that I learned the truth for myself—and it was liberating. Lack of promotion happens all the time. Once I realized that my experience was pretty typical,

I stopped wondering whether some flaw in my work was keeping the publisher from promoting it. *It had nothing to do with me.* With Appelbaum's advice in hand, I took my first tentative steps toward book promotion. And my books were the better for it.

BOOK PROMOTION FOR INTROVERTS

I own several volumes on how to promote books. I have to admit that I usually can't read more than a few pages of these because they make me feel like a complete slacker. There is no way I have the time, or the inclination, to do everything they suggest. Partly because I have a life; also, because I'm an introvert, and promoting a book is something that goes completely against my natural bent. You may feel the same way.

In Frank Oz's (1991) movie *What About Bob?*, an egotistical psychiatrist–author tells anyone who will listen that he's written a book (and conveniently keeps about 40 copies of it on the bookshelves in his office). For those of us in academia, selling things, even our own books, seems, well, tacky. It's like we've flipped open the trunk of our car and are shouting to passersby to "get 'em while they're hot."

Fortunately, there are ways you can promote your work without having to become someone you are not (Clemens, 2005). And promote you must. Promoting your book also contributes to the greater good. Keep in mind what you were trying to accomplish by writing the book in the first place. Your book isn't going to help anyone if no one knows it exists. So in this chapter and in chapter 13, I've summarized some painless ways to let others know about your work.

University Press Office

A resource that relatively few people take advantage of is the press office at their university or college. That's a shame, because this is a wonderful resource. Truthfully, I probably wouldn't have known about this either if the director of media relations at my university hadn't come for a visit to the lab where I work. Because our lab does a lot of research that has general interest (mostly in family violence research), she came to tell us how to work with the media.

What I particularly remember, and it transformed my thinking, was that when we allow the press office to publicize our work, it benefits both us and the university. For example, when granting agencies want to see the impact of their money, stories in local and national media are one type of measurable impact. So letting the press office know about your work is not an ego fest.

When to Call the Press Office

One thing that surprised me was how often the press office suggested that we call them. I had originally thought that I would only call if I had a major study come out or a new book. But their criteria are broader than that. They want to know whether we've gotten a promotion or new position. For example, when I was elected to the board of directors of a large parenting organization, the University of New Hampshire (UNH) press office issued a press release. They also want to know about major presentations or awards. If in doubt, ask them if they think your item is news-worthy and let them decide.

What the Press Office Can Do for You

When you contact the press office, they will work with you to write a press release. Often, they draft something and send it to you for your approval. They will then release it and let you know if there have been any inquiries from the press. When *The Well-Ordered Office* (Kendall-Tackett, 2005e) was released, I had many inquiries from the press and from freelance writers working on magazine articles as a result of the press release from UNH.

When a reporter or writer contacts you, get back to them promptly—within 24 hours is best. Have your press office time the release for when you will be avail-able to take calls. Whenever you complete an interview for print media, radio, or television, be sure to let the press office know. They need to keep stats on how many media contacts university faculty have had and may want a copy of relevant clippings.

I asked Erika Mantz, director of media relations at the UNH press office, to tell me some of the mistakes that faculty make with regard to the press office. She named two:

1. Avoiding the press! It is important to remember that talking with the media is a great opportunity, not something to fear. The media is in the business of telling stories, and faculty members have great stories to tell about their research and teaching. They also provide a great service by helping society understand and providing context and commentary about current and historical events of importance.

2. Not getting help. Most colleges and universities have a media relations office. Get to know it, and then use it. No one will tell you what to say, but they will share their expertise in an effort to make your experience a positive one. Also, don't be afraid to talk with colleagues you know have worked with the media.

In summary, your campus press office is a great resource for helping to promote your work. Call them and find out how you can start working together. Getting the word out about your work is the ultimate win–win.

What You Can Expect From Your Publisher

I think you have gathered by now that most publishers probably won't do as much as you would like them to in terms of marketing your book. There will probably not be lavish parties chock full of beautiful people drinking cocktails and clamoring for your autograph.

That happens sometimes, but it is rare for first-time authors or for authors of academic books in general.

That being said, your publisher can be helpful to you in some important ways. If you anticipate this, you will be in a position to take maximum advantage of the services they can offer you. Your publisher is likely to be so surprised and pleased that you are being proactive that they may be even more helpful.

Book Publicist

Most publishers have publicists or a designated marketing person who handles publicity for their books. You will probably be assigned to a publicist who will issue a press release about your book. This person will also field inquiries from the press and forward your contact information to reporters who call or write. Your publicist can also forward review copies of your book. Whenever I get requests for review copies, I forward them to my publicist. But remember, because you are not their only client, keep your expectations realistic about what the publicist will be able to do for you.

According to Earlita Chenault, the publicist I work with most often at New Harbinger Publications, your publicist is doing a lot behind the scenes before your book is even finished. About 3 to 5 months before your book's publication date, he or she prepares advance galleys to send out to library trade publications and other select long-lead media. These might include magazines that may be interested in interviewing you or reviewing or excerpting from your book around the time of publication.

Your book's publicist will usually create press kits and a list of media contacts. Press kits include a press release, author bio, suggested interview questions, raves from colleagues, and book excerpts or other supplemental information. Before mailing review copies, your publicist may produce postcards or e-mail blasts about your book. He or she will also make isolated pitches as opportunities present themselves.

I asked Chenault what authors can do to work more effectively with a book's publicity department and their book's publicist. This is what she said:

1. Check e-mail and voice mail regularly during the period directly preceding your book's publication and for 2 to 3 months afterward; a lot of times we'll get calls from editors and producers on a tight schedule, and if we can't deliver an author we've pitched, we all look a bit silly.

2. Please don't ask if we're going to pitch Oprah. We've heard of her and will pitch her and every other media professional that we think would be a good fit for you book.

3. Please don't contact us daily to ask if there has been anything new or to ask half a dozen questions. We will *definitely* contact you if anything has come up, and we want to answer every question. But if you can imagine getting 5 to 10 e-mails daily from authors who all want to ask 5 to 10 questions, you

can see the problem. We then have to ignore authors (which we hate to do, being softhearted individuals, every one of us) or neglect work on books, which none of us wants to do. The best thing is to consolidate all your questions into 1 to 2 e-mails a week. That way, if you contact us for something urgent, we are less likely to delay opening your e-mail.

4. And please, do not ask us anything outside the scope of our job (e.g., queries regarding your royalties, complimentary books, or the positioning of your book in Barnes & Noble) because we just don't know!

I also asked Chenault about the mistakes authors make regarding book publicity and what they can do to avoid them.

- Mistake Number 1 is thinking that the book comes out Monday, they're booked with Katie Couric for Tuesday, and on Oprah Wednesday. And if not, then the publicity department has failed and the book's a flop. Sometimes there is immediate interest in a book, but more often it starts slowly and hopefully builds. And if there is not media interest in the book, it could be for a number of reasons. But not for lack of trying on your publicist's part. Remember: Our jobs depend on our ability to get placements for your book!

- Another misconception is that if a magazine or show passes on the book and author, the publicist should just keep hounding them. This is not effective and is even counterproductive. Your publicist will not want to damage her future relationship with her contacts by trying to force-feed them a story. I will pitch a story–author–book one to three times if I've not had a response. But *no means no.*

After you've had any media contact, let your publicist know. Also, be sure to forward any copies of articles written about your book. Your publicist needs to keep stats about the work done on the author's behalf and also needs to keep the sales department aware of publicity of the book, which could affect advance sales and reorders. When you let them know what you are doing, you're helping them do their job well and are letting them know that your book is getting media attention.

Publicists will often want to know about any media experience you have. Particularly germane are radio and television appearances. When TV shows, such as the *Oprah Winfrey Show*, are looking for guests, they want to know that the person they are considering won't freeze when placed in front of a camera. I list my radio and television experience right on my curriculum vitae. And you might want to send video clips to the publicist if you have any.

It's also important for you to be forthright with your publicist. For example, if you have severe stage fright, mention that. It's better for the publicist to know about it now rather than after she has booked a TV appearance for you. Along these same lines, if you have a speech impediment of some kind, being interviewed on TV or the radio is going to be challenging. I have a physical disability, which doesn't impair my ability to speak in interviews. But I do need to make accommodations when I travel. I have to be forthright with conference organizers about my limitations. Sometimes, it's really a pain to have to divulge this kind of information. But in the long run, it's better to be forthright with what you can and cannot do. Along these same lines, if your publicist knows about your limitations, she can work to accommodate them and still give you a chance to make your best impression.

Marketing Questionnaire

When you were sent your contract, chances are you also received a *marketing questionnaire*. You usually turn this in with your completed manuscript, or you could send it in later. But this is something you should not neglect. In fact, you might even consider asking for one ahead of time if you are having trouble pinning down who your market is. Publicists and marketing departments like to get these as soon after the final manuscript is delivered as possible. Often, the questionnaires help them plan the promotional campaign for the book.

The marketing questionnaire will ask who should receive review copies. Are there journals that are key to your field? Are you a member of any key professional associations? What colleges are you a graduate of? Be sure to provide any contact information that your publisher needs to send copies of your book to these places.

Promotional Blurbs

A marketing questionnaire will also ask you for names of people who you could ask to review your book and write a few sentences that can be used on the back cover. These are known as *promotional blurbs*. When thinking about whom to ask, think about whose opinion is likely to sway readers' minds and convince them to buy your book. These people don't need to be celebrities, but it helps if they are people whose opinions make a difference in a particular field.

Before submitting someone's name, you might want to check with him or her. But if you are shy, don't worry about it. Your publisher will ask for you. Don't be discouraged if someone turns you down. People are very busy these days, and they may not have time to review your book and write a blurb for it. It doesn't meant that they don't like it.

As a general rule, I almost always will write a blurb for someone else. It's another one of those win–win situations. You give the author the material they need to promote their book. And you get your name and possibly the names of one or more of your own books listed on the back of someone else's book. Keep this in mind when you ask for blurbs: It's benefiting the blurber as much as the blurbee (and the blurber usually gets a free copy of your book). That being said, I'd recommend that you only write blurbs for books that you think are genuinely good. If you write blurbs for bad books, you lower your credibility.

Promotional Flyer

Be sure to ask your publisher for a promotional flyer. This is something you can pass out at conferences or give to people who are interested. Your publisher's graphic designer will often come up with something you can use. If possible, ask for both hard copies and an electronic version. The electronic version is nice if you want to e-mail it to people or post it on a Web site. If you are editing a book, you can also e-mail it to your contributing authors so that they can pass it out at any conferences they speak at or attend.

I've had a couple of instances where the flyer that the publisher produced was pretty bad. It was hard to read, and it wasn't very aesthetically pleasing (in my opinion). In those cases, I made my own flyer. I wrote a brief summary of the book content and included reader benefits ("After reading this book, you will be able to . . . "). Finally, I excerpted from any positive reviews that I received. Sometimes, if you have made your own flyer, you can show it to the graphic designer at your publisher, and they can make up something that you like better.

Ask to review any copy on your flyer before it goes to print. Like the back material, sometimes the copywriters are working from your book proposal rather than the finished product. Many things may have changed, including the title. And sometimes the description of the book doesn't really do it justice. Remember, you know your book better than anyone. What do you think are the key features? You can often work back and forth with the copywriter to come up with text that you both like.

WORKING WITH MEDIA

Both your publisher's publicist and your university press office will be generating interest in your book from the press. Your job is to be ready to field these media requests and give the information in a format they can use. Academics can be notoriously bad at this. But publicity can make the difference between success and failure of your book. Even if you aren't in it for the money, remember that you have something important to say, and you want as many people to know about your book as possible.

Over the past few years, I've given hundreds of interviews to reporters and freelance writers from across the United States and in other parts of the world. Because I work in a lab with a high profile in the child maltreatment field, any time there is a highly publicized child victimization case, we get calls. For example, my associates and I gave tons of interviews after the clergy abuse scandal broke in 2001–2002. I also get calls about trauma and depression, particularly in mothers. I even ended up on New Hampshire Public Television on September 11, 2001, talking about psychological trauma and looking pretty dazed myself from the day's events.

Because of the sheer volume of interviews I've given, I've had good ones and a few really bad ones. Even if the interview doesn't go as well as you would like, it is not the end of the world. I've had situations in which reporters have written the exact opposite of what I've said. It wasn't great. But neither was it a catastrophe. One of my worst interview experiences was when I returned to my college campus for a series of invited lectures. A reporter from the local paper interviewed me about depression in new mothers. What she wrote in the article was pure gibberish. I mean, the sentences literally made no sense. I was horrified. What's worse, the gibberish was supposedly a quote. And there was a large picture of me, just in case people missed my name.

Another time, I was interviewed for a Japanese business newspaper about *The Well-Ordered Office*. After chatting for a while, the interviewer asked, "So if someone has messy desk, they have mental illness?" I think most of us would be in big trouble if that were true. Talk about being "lost in translation"! I believe we got it straightened out, but I'm not sure, because the article was in Japanese. Fortunately, my Japanese sister-in-law, Michiko, thought the article was nice and assured me that it said nothing about mental illness.

Generally speaking, my experiences with media have been positive. I've been interviewed by writers from many national magazines, including *Better Homes and Gardens, Woman's Day, Family Circle, First for Women, Glamour, Fitness, Shape, Fit Pregnancy, Baby Talk, American Baby, Parents,* and *Parenting.* These magazines fact-check everything, and after my interviews, I've had the opportunity to correct words attributed to me. Even if I don't make changes, I'm glad that they are checking to make sure people in their articles are quoted correctly.

One time, a national magazine sent a photographer and make-up artist to my house to shoot some pictures to accompany an article they were writing. The article was about things people could do around their homes to lift their spirits during the long winter months. We talked about some ways women could easily incorporate bright colors into their homes. One suggestion I offered (among many) was to keep a bowl of colorful fruit on their dining room tables. I made sure to tell the reporter that I don't do this because my dining room table is right next to my wood stove. If I did this, in a couple of days, I'd have compote. But the magazine decided that they wanted a picture of me with the fruit.

Before the big day, they sent me a list of what not to wear, which pretty much included my entire wardrobe. The stylist spent about 45 minutes on my hair and make-up—something I never do. When she was finished, my kids wanted to know who this poofyhaired stranger was. After all that, the magazine ended up only using a head shot—sans fruit. I haven't looked at magazine photos the same way since.

Being Interviewed for Magazine Articles

I asked Teresa Pitman, whom you met in chapter 8, to share some of her experiences in interviewing academics for her articles. Pitman writes for *Today's Parent*, Canada's largest parenting magazine. She told me that university professors are one of her major resources. But she also identified some of the challenges that she has encountered. What she says may help you think about ways you can communicate more effectively with people who will write about your work.

- Sometimes professors don't understand the tight timelines journalists are typically working under. With a magazine, I usually have about 6 weeks total to research and write the article, but sometimes it is much less. I may have already used up part of that 6 weeks just tracking down a suitable person to interview, so if they don't get back to me for another 2 weeks, it will be too late.
- Some professors are very narrowly focused on a particular research project and don't want to discuss anything broader. I do understand this, but I always appreciate the person who is willing to speculate on how the research might be applied to help parents or who has a broader understanding

of the field and can make connections to other research that has been done.

- Some have trouble speaking in language that my readers will be able to understand. I usually end up dealing with this by not using direct quotes, just paraphrasing. But I always appreciate it when they can simplify and say things using easily understood words.

- Sometimes people want to see the article before I submit it. This is not considered okay by editors (and journalists). I will sometimes send people their quotes (not the full article) if they really insist. We do have fact-checkers, so I let them know that the person will call and go over things with them. I have (rarely) had someone who, when the fact-checker called, wanted all of his or her quotes changed, sometimes quite drastically. This has happened even when I've done the interview by e-mail so had everything clearly printed out and quoted it exactly. That is frustrating for me, because it means I have to rewrite the article to fit with the new quotes.

- If I can also add a couple of good things: I have a number of academic experts whom I return to over and over because they are so good at explaining complicated research or issues in terms that ordinary parents can understand. Many of them are also helpful because they will tell me about new research in their field that is coming up, suggest future article ideas to me, suggest someone else I should contact, and so on.

Suggestions for Interviews

Like anything else, working with media gets easier with time and practice. Here are some suggestions to help you prepare for interviews (Clemens, 2005).

- Be concise and prepared. Think through the most important findings or other information you want to convey and say them in one sentence or less. A sound bite is about 20 seconds. You are less likely to be cut off or edited if you have a concise answer. Also be prepared to say why you wrote the book and what need it fulfills.

- If a reporter calls, and now is not a good time to be interviewed, reschedule your interview for a better time. Erika Mantz, the director of the UNH press office, suggested the following:

  If you think you need time to prepare for an interview, ask about the reporter's deadline and tell them you'll call them back before then. Reporters are often working on tight deadlines; respect that, and always return the call. It's okay to ask the reporter what questions they want answered, but don't try to memorize your responses. Organize your thoughts and know what your key messages are; ask your media relations office for help if you need it.

  Be aware, however, that the reporter may not have time to give you too long of a delay. But sometimes even waiting a couple of hours can give you a chance to gather your thoughts and think about what you need to say.

- Be prepared to state how your research, book, or other venture is relevant to people in the real world. Mantz also suggested you avoid using field-specific jargon and that you use real-world examples whenever possible.

- If you don't understand the question or don't know the answer, don't be afraid to say so. Be honest with reporters about what you know and don't know.

- Don't ask a reporter to send you a copy of the story before it is printed. As much as you'd like to have the final say about quotations attributed to you, according to Mantz, it's not appropriate for you to ask to see the text before it is printed: "You're not their editor. Instead, ask them to read back your quotes, to ensure you got your point across." You could also ask if the article is going to be fact-checked before publication.

- When being interviewed on television, always ask the interviewer where they want you to look. Generally, they will have you look at them, not the camera. But ask just to be sure.

- If your interview is televised, find out when it will be aired, and tape the program. Some scouts for the big talk shows want to see tapes of you on television to make sure that you are not boring. Save these. Fortunately, more and more stations are putting their shows online. If they do, you can refer interested scouts to these sites with the appropriate dates.

Publicity Events

Depending on the topic of your book, a reporter might also suggest a publicity event. I had an event last summer that generated a lot of local press for my book, *The Well-Ordered Office*. Nate Pardue, a reporter from *Foster's Daily Democrat*, came up with the idea that we have a "messy office" contest, and the winner got *me* for an office makeover! As you can imagine, I wasn't exactly looking forward to it. I e-mailed Chenault, my publicist at New Harbinger, and she thought it was a great idea (traitor!). I finally agreed.

They ran the contest, and the winner was the office of the local Hallmark store in downtown Dover, New Hampshire. The first day I went just to talk with them and figure out what we needed to do. I walked into the store, and there was a huge whiteboard with "Welcome Kathleen Kendall-Tackett. We love you!" How could I not like them after such a nice greeting?

Their office did need a lot of work (remember, it *won* a messy office competition). I worked with them for 3 days. While we worked, the paper sent a photographer down a couple more times to take pictures of our progress. The store owners, Ann Goodman and Janet Berry, said that lots of people stopped in to look at their office and comment on the story. When we finished, there was a large article in the Sunday paper, complete with pictures of me and my book. The whole project turned out to be a lot of fun, and I was glad I did it. So I guess that I would recommend that you consider participating in something similar if your topic warrants it.

Most recently, I was asked to send a copy of *The Hidden Feelings of Motherhood* (Kendall-Tackett, 2005c) to the TV show *Law & Order: Special Victims Unit*. They wanted to use it as a prop. After I had sent the book, my teenage son, Ken, who loves all things *Law & Order*, asked if I knew what they were going to say about my book. In other words, was someone going to say that they became a psychopathic killer after reading *The Hidden Feelings of Motherhood*? Fortunately, my publisher had the presence of mind to ask and told me that the plot line was just fine. When the show finally aired, they said the author's name was "Kendall" instead of "Kendall-Tackett." But several friends saw it and recognized it as my book.

CONCLUSION

Working with media is a great way to get your book before the public. Your university press office and book's publicist are your gateway to the media. Be sure to work with them, thank them for their efforts on your behalf, and don't be a pest. Think about what you want to say ahead of time, and relax. No one expects you to be slick. But they do want you to be clear and engaging. Interviews can be a lot of fun. Think of them as opportunities to teach the public about your work. And if you can communicate well, you'll find lots of people interested in what you have to say.

13

Book Promotion II:
Seminars and Web Marketing

Nearly all the great writers you've ever read did one thing
besides writing: They shared. Isn't it about time
you shared your work too? Step out from the shadows.
The world is waiting.
—Jack Clemens (2005, p. 27)

In the previous chapter, I shared some strategies for working with media to help promote your book. In this chapter, I'll describe some other strategies for promoting work, including seminars and lectures and creating a presence on the Web.

Seminars and Lectures

One of the most natural ways for you to promote your work is by teaching seminars on your topic. This is something I do frequently. Teaching seminars was something that gradually evolved as I continued to write. When I first started, I only made 3 or 4 presentations per year. Now I give more than 50 presentations in a year.

Having been both a speaker and conference organizer, I can tell you that there's plenty of room out there for good speakers. If you think you might enjoy this type of work, then start with some local meetings and see how it goes. Conference organizers are always on the lookout for speakers with something interesting to say who can also present well. There's no reason that can't be you.

Book Sales at Conferences

The more experience you have as a speaker, the more you can charge. Even if you are not paid well for presenting at a conference, if you can sell your books, it will probably be worth your while. I'm often willing to reduce my speaking fee if I can sell books. Book sales can be substantial at meetings. Speaking also gives you a great opportunity to pass out your book flyers. Ask conference organizers if you can send the book flyers ahead of time so they can be added to the attendee packets. If not, bring them along and either pass them out yourself or have your session monitor (if there is one) pass them out for you.

Before meetings, ask the conference coordinators whether they would prefer for you to bring the books or if they want to order them directly. Whatever they decide, make it easy for them to get your books. I recently developed a sheet that tells conference bookstore managers where they can order my books. I list the title and ISBN number for each book, the publisher's telephone number, the discount offered, and the name of the person they are supposed to contact. (Sometimes, for conferences to receive a discount, conference organizers need to go through the marketing department rather than regular customer service.) The point, again, is to make it as easy as possible for people to get your books. It's good for both of you.

Speaking Basics

Because I speak at a lot of conferences, I've had a chance to see what works and what doesn't and to fine tune my approach.

List of Your Session Topics

The first thing I'd suggest is that you streamline all of the information that conference organizers will need from you. This includes a listing of all your conference sessions that you can present, a bio, a bibliography for each session, and your outlines and objectives that must be submitted for continuing education (CE) credits. You might consider making this information available on your Web site so you can refer conference organizers there to get the information they need.

If you present on more than one topic, put together a listing of all your possible sessions with a title and a three- to four-sentence description of what the session entails for each. Conference planners can use this description in their conference brochures. Remember, people will decide about whether they will attend your seminar based on the description in the brochure. So try to make it enticing. What will they learn if they attend your workshop? What are the benefits to them? In Exhibit 13.1, I've listed descriptions of three sessions that I regularly provide. My full list contains 11 different sessions: 6 for professionals and 5 for a general audience.

Sessions for Continuing Education Credits

CE credits are for people with professional licenses that they must maintain with ongoing education. Examples of professionals who may need continuing education credits include clinical psychologists and social workers, nurses, physicians, or other allied health professionals. Organizations that offer CE credits include hospitals, educational institutes, and individual companies and organizations that have been accredited to offer these units through a relevant professional organization.

Know that for each CE session, you will eventually have to produce an outline of content with objectives and a complete bibliography. You write objectives in terms of what the attendee will be able to do after they attend your session. For example, here are the objectives for my "Depression in New Mothers" double session:

1. Describe the symptoms of postpartum depression, how often it occurs, and the consequences of postpartum depression for both mothers and babies.

EXHIBIT 13.1 Conference Topics

Depression in New Mothers I: Causes and Consequences.
There are many factors that make mothers vulnerable to depression. These include physiological factors such as pain, fatigue, and inflammation; negative birth experiences; infants' difficult temperament or health issues; lack of social support; low income; and a woman's history of prior depression and/or childhood abuse. This session will cover common myths about postpartum depression, the factors that make mothers vulnerable, and why depression is bad for both mothers and babies. **Publications available:** *Depression in New Mothers* (book), *Postpartum depression and the breastfeeding mother* (LLLI LC Unit). **75–120 minutes.**

Depression in New Mothers II: Treatment Options for Breastfeeding Mothers. There are a number of scientifically proven treatments for depression, and most are compatible with breastfeeding. This session summarizes research findings on diet, exercise, Omega-3 fatty acids, SAMe, St. John's Wort, psychotherapy, and antidepressant medications and describes the implications of each for breastfeeding. **Publications available:** *Depression in New Mothers* (book), *Postpartum depression and the breastfeeding mother* (LLLI LC Unit). **75–120 minutes.**

Note. **Depression in New Mothers I and II** can also be offered as a double session.

Breastfeeding and the Sexual Abuse Survivor: Can events from childhood influence a woman's current mothering experience? This session will provide you with the latest research on how past abuse can affect a woman's body, mind and spirit and what she can do to overcome these effects. This session will also provide some specific strategies to help with abuse issues for yourself or others you work with. **Publications available:** *Depression in New Mothers* (book), *Hidden Feelings of Motherhood* (book), *Health Consequences of Abuse in the Family* (book), *Breastfeeding and the sexual abuse survivor* (LLLI LC Module). **75–90 minutes.**

2. Identify the factors that contribute to depression during the year after childbirth.
3. Describe the role of social support in preventing depression.
4. List treatment options available for new mothers.

I keep the outline forms for each session I teach, so it is fairly straightforward to adjust the times (although a typical session is 75 minutes), change the title and conference location, and submit it. Having been on both sides of the fence, I'd urge you to get your materials to your conference organizers promptly. Don't make them chase you. I've had several conference organizers tell me that I'm always the first to get my materials to them. And this has led to a lot of other speaking engagements for me. Conference coordinators talk to each other. And this is one question they always ask.

Bring a Bio

This is something that you may not think of, but if you bring a short bio, you'll be happier with your introductions. Relying on what people decide to pull off of your curriculum vitae is risky. I've had people say the oddest things, to the point where I wanted to laugh out loud. I was recently introduced as one of the founders of La Leche League. Considering that this organization was founded 3 years before I was born, I'd say that this was quite a feat.

Be Careful With Portable Microphones

Just a quick reminder to be careful when you are wearing a portable microphone. You don't want to be broadcasting your conversation in the hall to a room full of people. And definitely make sure the microphone is off before you hit the restroom! (I had an audiovisual tech remind me of this just this week. Apparently, it had been a problem at their facility.) I've never done that (fortunately!), but I know several people who have. So pay attention to what you do. If in doubt, take your microphone off completely before you leave the podium.

Use Readable PowerPoint Design Templates

PowerPoint has lots of lovely background designs. But not all of them make for good presentations. Before using that fabulous template with lime-green type, try it out on a big screen. Chances are you will discover that it is almost impossible to read at any distance. It's better to find that out now than when you have 400 eyes turned your way. Remember that just because a template comes with a certain color font doesn't mean you need to use it. You can change the color under the "Font" command. I've found that the best slide backgrounds are the highest contrast. A lot of my presentations have a black background with white writing.

Something else to mention. Academics often put way too much text on a PowerPoint slide. Just because

PowerPoint allows you to do that doesn't mean it is a good idea. A few years ago, I wrote a newsletter article for the divisions within the American Psychological Association on making presentations accessible to people with disabilities. One thing I recommended was never using anything smaller than 24-point type. That's good advice in general. When the font gets smaller than that, it's more than people can take in. And what's the point of putting up something people can't read?

I was at a really ridiculous talk a few years ago. The speaker started off by putting up a slide of a horse, but kept referring to it as a cow. I was sitting with my friend, Gwen Vesenka, who has a PhD in biology. I said to her, "That looks like a horse. Isn't that a horse? Is that a cow that looks like a horse?" I thought with her advanced education, she could shed light on the whole horse–cow distinction. She assured me that it was indeed a horse. Finally, after about 10 minutes of talking about a cow, the speaker turned around, saw her slide and said, "Oh, that's a horse!"

Her next slide was even worse! She put up a table that probably came from one of her papers. The font was no bigger than 12 points. Then she told us to not bother reading it because all the text was in Norwegian! *Then why was it up there?* This presentation was the plenary session of a major scientific meeting—and it was a disaster. Promise me that you will never do that.

Consider Buying Your Own Equipment

If you do a lot of speaking, you might consider buying your own LCD projector. I had to learn this the hard way. Renting equipment for a meeting is very expensive for conference organizers—often topping $600 a day per room. For smaller meetings, that cost is often prohibitive. So people will borrow projectors, and who knows what you will get? I've had people drag out some ancient projector, built circa 1956, that their husband's friend's uncle was able to borrow from work, and they'll say something like, "I hope you know how to run this." Having been through some PowerPoint disasters and lived to tell the tale, I can say that it's nice to have my own projector. If I speak at a hospital or a big conference, I usually don't need it. But it's come in handy at many a small meeting and is one less thing for me to worry about.

Something else you might also consider is asking conference organizers to print handouts from your slides. Many will do this anyway. But it's a good backup for you. If push comes to shove, you can lecture off the notes.

The Naked Truth About Book Signings

The next form of promotion I'd like to discuss is book signing. Aspiring authors often dream of book signings, with people wrapped around the block, waiting for them to sign their book. I've had the opportunity to do lots of book signings—so many, I've literally lost count. Most have been good, but they vary quite a bit. Fortunately, there are some things you can do to make your signings more successful.

Know That Sometimes No One Comes

I'm really grateful to other writers for sharing honestly what their book signing experiences have been like. Some can be pretty bad, and it's helpful to know that bad signings happen to good people. Author Anne Lamott, in her classic writing book *Bird by Bird* (1994), described going to a signing at a bookstore where the only attendees were the store employees and a homeless man. And the homeless man didn't like Brie.

I've had signings like that as well. At one, I was propped up on a stool with a pen in my hand at my publisher's booth, waiting for someone to swing by and buy a book for me to sign. There were several thousand people at that conference, and even very well-known authors were having trouble attracting people. I hadn't spoken at the conference, and the conference wasn't really on topic of that book. It was the longest hour of my life. Another time I was placed at a card table at the entrance of a bookstore. People coming into the store got very good at avoiding eye contact with me.

Now that I've told you about some bad experiences, let me tell you about a good one. I was speaking at a conference once in Virginia. The conference organizers had sold out of the three different books of mine that they were offering. I had some books with me and brought them over the next morning before leaving for the airport. Fortunately, I was a little early. As I dropped the books off, a small mob of people gathered, asking me to sign their books. I stood there for over an hour and never even got my coat off. In thinking about good versus bad book signings, there are a few details that can make the difference.

Sign Books at Conferences Where You Speak. I have found that few people are willing to buy books just because you are sitting there with a pen. If they hear what you have to say and like it, chances are they will want a copy of your book. Even if you do a more traditional bookstore book signing, ask if you can do a brief presentation. I recently did a bookstore event that was offered in conjunction with a local hospital for National Depression Screening Day. I wasn't too optimistic, based on my past experiences. But I prepared a brief presentation and was delighted when the seating area started filling up with moms and babies. And I sold (and signed) a lot of books.

Give Them Something They Can Use. When making a presentation, try to give them some information they can use. Not all topics will lend themselves to this. But yours might, and it will add value to your session. Even if they don't buy your book that day, they may buy one later, or tell someone they know about it.

Don't Be Afraid to Stack the Deck. If you are asked to do a regular book signing, especially if local, ask people you know to go. This isn't cheating; it's smart.

People are unlikely to venture over if they will be the only one in the audience. Would you? If there are a few people there, then others will feel safe about joining the group and won't worry about being pressured to buy a book.

When Signing, Don't Talk While Writing. Book signings are no time for multitasking. Try to concentrate when you are writing or you are apt to make embarrassing spelling errors (just trust me on this, okay?). When you make those types of mistakes, you may have trouble convincing your audience that you is a writer, if you catch my drift.

Find Out Something About Them. Even though this event is "all about you," it will be boring if you approach it that way for long. People have come to see you, but this is a good opportunity for you to find out about them. I've had a lot of really interesting conversations this way, and it's a great way to keep in touch with the needs of your target audience.

Spell Names Correctly. After you find out who the book is for, be sure to get the correct spelling of the person's name. If it is for a conference attendee, look at their name tag (and ask if that is the correct spelling). If it is for a friend, have them spell that name, too. Even common names have lots of variations, and some parents love saddling their children with oddly spelled monikers, just so they stand out.

Write Something Nice. I was once at a book signing with several other authors. The man next to me was one of the leaders in the field. He had a new book out, and as several copies of it came through the line, I thought it looked like a good book. When I had a break, I slipped over to the bookstore and bought a copy. When he had a break, I asked if he would sign mine. He leaned over, looked at my name tag, and wrote "To Kathleen," signed his name and wrote the date. I don't know what got into me, but I started fake crying and said, "This is so moving. I'll cherish it always." My friends were just horrified because he was such a big shot. He, on the other hand, seemed amused, and said, "Give me that book." He amended his signature to say, "I will cherish this book signing always." If he was mad, he didn't show it, and he wrote the foreword for one of my later books.

When I sign books, I try to write a sentence or two before signing my name. For example, if I know a woman is a new mom, I might say, "My very best wishes in your mothering adventures." If someone has worked with moms and babies for a while, I might say something like, "Thanks for all you do for mothers and babies." It's also nice to use book signings as opportunities to encourage the people you meet. So think of a couple of things you can write that would be meaningful to people who are reading your books.

CREATING A WEB PRESENCE

The Internet gives lots of opportunities for individuals to market their books, provide information, and receive feedback from readers. There are two easy ways for you to create a presence on the Web. You can create a Web site for your books. And you can boost your Amazon.com sales by soliciting reviews. I've described both of these below.

Book Web Sites

A Web site for your book is a great way to advertise your book and provide additional information. My most recent Web site was for *Breastfeeding Made Simple* (Mohrbacher & Kendall-Tackett, 2005; http://www.BreastfeedingMadeSimple.com). My coauthor and I specifically described the Web site we would create to accompany the book when we pitched it, and it became a major selling point. We could offer lots more information on the site than we could squeeze into our book. And we were able to offer something that no one else had: animated pictures showing moms how to latch their babies onto the breast. This was a significant advantage, because it's often very difficult to teach this to moms using only static pictures—the kind in most books.

The other thing we were able to provide on the *Breastfeeding Made Simple* Web site was materials mothers could print out and give to their doctors. We included position papers from the American Academy of Pediatrics and the Academy of Breastfeeding Medicine. We also included numerous links to other sites, handouts that other professionals have given us access to, and some general information compiled about breastfeeding by the U.S. government. The more content you have, the more likely people are to return to your site.

As soon as we all agreed on a title for the book, I reserved the domain name and paid a small monthly fee to reserve our access to it. Prominently displayed is a graphic of our book cover, with a link to Amazon. com so that people can purchase it. There is also author information, including our curricula vitae and speaking schedules.

Finally, have a way for readers to contact you. And be sure to write them back to thank them for comments or suggestions. Collect any e-mail addresses of people who write to you so you can send them updates on any new books or related products.

Increasing Sales on Amazon.com

Amazon.com has been a boon to both small publishers and consumers. It's a place to get just about anything, and that's good news for you and your books. You don't want to be idle about your Amazon.com sales, however. One thing you can do is make sure that you have book reviews for each of your books. People are less likely to buy unreviewed books, and that lack of sales is reflected in a high Amazon.com rank (as mentioned in chapter 10, low numbers are the ones you want).

If you are thinking about reviewers, you can start with people you know. This is especially good if they don't share your last name or don't live in the same part of the country. For example, it would be pretty strange for me to have only reviewers from New Hampshire. If you ask someone to write you a review, provide them with a copy of the book. Then stay out of it! To keep things legitimate, don't correct or in any way edit their reviews. It may help if you tell potential reviewers that this is your intention so they don't feel pressured to say only nice things (although you hope that they would say mostly nice things).

Another source of reviewers is readers you don't know but who tell you that they loved your book. Ask if they would be willing to write an online review. Often, they are flattered that you asked and happy to help you. These types of reviews may be even better. The main thing you want to do is create buzz about your book. From there, others will eventually chime in. But take responsibility for getting things moving in that direction.

What Amazon.com Numbers Mean

I still vividly remember what it was like to see a book of mine on Amazon.com for the first time. I was out of town, but periodically checking e-mail. One message was from Amazon. It said "Dear Kathy Kendall-Tackett, Since you have bought such and such books on depression in mothers, you might be interested in a new book by Dr. Kathleen Kendall-Tackett. . . . "

I followed the link to their site, and I saw that *The Hidden Feelings of Motherhood* (Kendall-Tackett,

2001) had a rank of 1,195. I had no idea what that meant. By coincidence, I happened to catch Jeff Bezos (founder of Amazon.com) on C-SPAN a couple of nights later. And he explained it all. According to Bezos, any book with a ranking below 10,000 was considered a "best seller," and those rankings changed every hour (so you may not remain a "best seller" for long). Books ranked 10,001 to 100,000 were the next tier. Those rankings were changed every 24 hours. The final ranking tier was 100,001 and up. Those numbers were changed once a month at that time. (More recently, those numbers also seem to change every 24 hours.) Most academic books fall into the 100,001 and up category. It doesn't mean they are bad or even that they lack influence. It simply means that book is not moving the same number of copies as books with a wider audience.

The lowest Amazon.com rank I've had so far was 960 for *The Well-Ordered Home* (Kendall-Tackett, 2003). But I should warn you that you can make yourself crazy checking these. I look every week or 2 but try not to peek more often than that. And it's very difficult to know how those numbers correspond to number of books sold. Apparently, that's a closely guarded secret. But low numbers are definitely the ones you want.

CONCLUSION

Book promotion needn't be an ego fest. You are providing useful information to people who would benefit from it. Teaching and offering information on the Web are great low-stress ways to reach your target audience. And if you happen to sell a lot of books along the way, then good for you!

Some Final Thoughts

So my friends, our time together has come to an end. In closing, I'd like to leave you with two final thoughts.

Not everyone will be thrilled with your writing efforts, especially in the beginning, and they may tell you "no." Keep in mind that everyone goes through this at one time or another. Try not to get discouraged, and make sure that you get some social support. If you knock on enough doors, eventually one will open. You'll be glad that you kept trying.

Also, don't be afraid to ask for help. Sometimes we don't get very far in our efforts because we assume that we have to do everything on our own. If you do nothing else, please disabuse yourself of this belief. No man (or woman) is an island. We can't do everything alone, and our final product will be so much better if we don't. If you don't know how to do something, ask someone who does. He or she will probably be happy to help. If the first person says no, ask someone else. This might mean talking to your press office, your reference librarian, or even your students. And be sure to reciprocate when you can. It's worth stepping outside of your comfort zone for.

I hope that you find writing as exhilarating as I have. You are now equipped to change the world one reader at a time. Get out there and make me proud!

References

Ambrose, S. (2002). *To America: Personal reflections of an historian.* New York: Simon & Schuster.

American Psychiatric Association. (2000). *Diagnostic and statistical manual of mental disorders* (4th ed., text revision). Washington, DC: Author.

American Psychological Association. (2001). *Publication manual of the American Psychological Association* (5th ed.). Washington, DC: Author.

Appelbaum, J. (1998). *How to get happily published* (5th ed.). New York: Collins.

Aslett, D., & Cartaino, C. (2001). *Get organized, get published! 225 ways to make time for success.* Cincinnati, OH: Writer's Digest Books.

Bardsley, M. (2005, February). Michele takes Manhattan. *Writer's Digest,* 30–34.

Barnson-Hayward, S. (2005, July). Caution: Parent at work. *Writer's Digest,* 40–41.

Bell, J. S. (2005, February). Three secrets of suspense. *Writer's Digest,* 20–21.

Bentley, T. (2005, August). Crafting a first-person essay. *Writer's Digest,* 37–39.

Bete, T. (2005, February). How to write funny. *Writer's Digest*, 35–37.

Bly, R. (2005, October). Costly mistakes. *Writer's Digest*, 22–23.

Brogan, K. S. (2005). *2005 Writer's Market*. Cincinnati, OH: Writer's Digest Books.

Burns, D. D. (1980). *Feeling good: The new mood therapy*. New York: Avon.

Burns, D. D. (1990). *The feeling good handbook*. New York: Plume.

Cheney, T. A. R. (2001). *Writing creative nonfiction: Fiction techniques for crafting great nonfiction*. Berkeley, CA: Ten Speed Press.

Cheney, T. A. R. (2005). *Getting the words right* (2nd ed.). Cincinnati, OH: Writer's Digest Books.

Clausen, J. (2001). *Too lazy to work, too nervous to steal: How to have a great life as a freelance writer*. Cincinnati, OH: Writer's Digest Books.

Clemens, J. (2005, July). The wimp's guide to promoting your work. *Writer's Digest*, 24–27.

Connor, T. (2006, January). What's the deal? *Writer's Digest*, 54–55.

Covey, S. R. (2004). *The 7 habits of highly effective people: Powerful lessons in personal change*. New York: Free Press.

Elliot, S. (2005). *The grassfire effect: How one small spark can change your world*. Nashville, TN: Broadman and Holman.

Feiertag, J., & Cupito, M. C. (2004). Writer's Market *companion* (2nd ed.). Cincinnati, OH: Writer's Digest Books.

Fishman, S. (2004a). *The copyright handbook: How to protect and use written works.* Berkeley, CA: NOLO Press.

Fishman, S. (2004b). *The public domain: How to find and use copyright-free writings, music, art & more.* Berkeley, CA: NOLO Press.

Fletcher, J. B. (2005, November). Squelch your inner censor. *Writer's Digest,* 36–37.

Fryxell, D. A. (2004). *Write faster, write better: Time-saving techniques for writing great fiction and nonfiction.* Cincinnati, OH: Writer's Digest Books.

Fryxell, D. A. (2005, September). Dropping in your data. *Writer's Digest,* 22–23.

Gawande, A. (2002). *Complications: A surgeon's notes on an imperfect science.* New York: Picador.

Glatzer, J. (2005a, September). What editors won't tell you (but we will). *Writer's Digest,* 27–30.

Glatzer, J. (2005b, July). Nice work—just change everything. *Writer's Digest,* 42–44.

Glatzer, J. (2005c). Popular magazines: How to break in. In K. S. Brogan (Ed.), *2005 Writer's Market* (pp. 17–19). Cincinnati, OH: Writer's Digest Books.

Hale, T. (2006). *Medications and mothers' milk* (12th ed.). Amarillo, TX: Hale Publishing.

Hayden, G. M. (2005, July). Paying your dues. *Writer's Digest,* 58.

Hewitt, H. (2005). *Blog: Understanding the information reformation that's changing your world*. Nashville, TN: Nelson.

James-Enger, K. (2005, December). The 2 sides of freelancing: Which writing suits you best, articles or books? Your goals, lifestyle, and personality are all factors. *The Writer*, 31–33.

Jones, G., Steketee, R. W., Black, R. E., Bhutta, Z. A., Morris, S. S., & the Bellagio Child Survival Study Group. (2003). How many child deaths can we prevent this year? *The Lancet, 362*, 65–71.

Kendall-Tackett, K. A. (2001). *The hidden feelings of motherhood: Coping with mothering stress, depression and burnout*. Oakland, CA: New Harbinger.

Kendall-Tackett, K. A. (2002). Making peace with your birth experience. *New Beginnings, 19*, 44–47.

Kendall-Tackett, K. A. (2003). *The well-ordered home: Organizing techniques for inviting serenity into your life*. Oakland, CA: New Harbinger.

Kendall-Tackett, K. A. (Ed.). (2004). *Health consequences of abuse in the family: A clinical guide for evidence-based practice*. Washington, DC: American Psychological Association.

Kendall-Tackett, K. A. (2005a). *Depression in new mothers: Causes, consequences, and treatment options*. Binghamton, NY: Haworth.

Kendall-Tackett, K. A. (2005b). *The handbook of women, stress and trauma*. New York: Taylor & Francis.

Kendall-Tackett, K. A. (2005c). *The hidden feelings of motherhood: Coping with mothering stress, depression and burnout* (2nd ed.). Amarillo, TX: Hale Publishing.

Kendall-Tackett, K. A. (2005d). New research on postpartum depression. *Leaven, 41,* 75–79.

Kendall-Tackett, K. A. (2005e). *The well-ordered office.* Oakland, CA: New Harbinger.

Kilpatrick, W. K. (1983). *Psychological seduction: The failure of modern psychology.* Nashville, TN: Thomas Nelson.

King, S. (2000). *On writing: A memoir of the craft.* New York: Scribner.

Kirsch, J. (1995). *Kirsch's handbook of publishing law.* Los Angeles: Acrobat Books.

Klems, B. (2005a, August). Blogging away rights? *Writer's Digest,* 23.

Klems, B. (2005b, August). The evolution of self-publishing. *Writer's Digest,* 2–11.

Koverola, C., & Panchanadeswaran, S. (2004). Domestic violence interventions with women of color: Intersection of victimization and cultural diversity. In K. Kendall-Tackett (Ed.), *Health consequences of abuse in the family: A clinical guide for evidence-based practice* (pp. 45–62). Washington, DC: American Psychological Association.

Lamott, A. (1994). *Bird by bird: Some instructions on writing and life.* New York: Anchor.

Lucado, M. (2005). *Cure for the common life: Living in your sweet spot.* Nashville, TN: W Publishing Group.

Lyon, E. (2003). *A writer's guide to non-fiction.* New York: Perigee.

McCullough, D. (2005). *1776.* New York: Simon & Schuster.

McGee-Cooper, A., with Tramell, D. (1994). *Time management for unmanageable people.* New York: Bantam.

Meanwell, M. (2004). *The wealthy writer.* Cincinnati, OH: Writer's Digest Books.

Mohrbacher, N., & Kendall-Tackett, K. A. (2005). *Breastfeeding made simple: Seven natural laws for nursing mothers.* Oakland, CA: New Harbinger.

Mohrbacher, N., & Stock, J. (2003). *The breastfeeding answer book.* Schaumburg, IL: La Leche League International.

Morgenstern, J. (2004). *Making work work: New strategies for surviving and thriving at the office.* New York: Fireside.

Morris, J. M. (2005, July). Bringing life stories to life. *Writer's Digest,* 37–39.

Niles, E. (2005). *Some writers deserve to starve: 31 brutal truths about the publishing industry.* Cincinnati, OH: Writer's Digest Books.

Noonan, P. (2001). *When character was king: A story of Ronald Reagan.* New York: Penguin.

Notbohm, E. (2006, January). Free isn't always a four-letter word. *The Writer,* 45–46.

Oz, F. (Director). (1991). *What about Bob?* [Motion picture]. United States: Buena Vista Home Entertainment.

Paine, T. (2004). The crisis. In B. Kuklick (Ed.), *Paine political writings* (pp. 49–56). Cambridge, England: Cambridge University Press. (Original work published 1776)

Poynter, D. (2003). *Writing non-fiction: Turning thoughts into books* (3rd ed.). Santa Barbara, CA: Para Publishing.

Poynter, D. (2004). *Dan Poynter's ParaPublishing.com: Statistics.* Retrieved March 6, 2007, from http://www.parapublishing.com/sites/para/resources/statistics.cfm

Poynter, D. (2006). *The self-publishing manual: How to write, print, and sell your own book* (15th ed.). Santa Barbara, CA: Para Press.

Rogers, B. H. (2005, November). Cloistered writing: When you need a dose of discipline, take a writing retreat—At home. *The Writer,* 15–18.

Ross, T., & Ross, M. (2002). *The complete guide to self-publishing: Everything you need to know to write, publish, promote, and sell your own book* (4th ed.). Cincinnati, OH: Writer's Digest Books.

Rubie, P. (2003). *Telling the story: How to write and sell narrative nonfiction.* New York: Quill.

Scott, R. (2005, May). The work habits of highly successful writers. *Writer's Digest,* 33–37.

Sellers, H. (2005). *Page after page: Discover the confidence and passion you need to start writing and keep writing (no matter what!)*. Cincinnati, OH: Writer's Digest Books.

Smokler, K. (2005, October). The future is now. *Writer's Digest*, 10–11.

Spiegel, R. (2005). Online opportunities: Live the freelance life online. In K. S. Brogan (Ed.), *2005 Writer's Market* (pp. 67–70). Cincinnati, OH: Writer's Digest Books.

Stowe, H. B. (1982). *Uncle Tom's Cabin*. New York: Bantam Classics. (Original work published 1852)

Strunk, W., Jr., & White, E. B. (1979). *The elements of style* (3rd ed.). Boston: Allyn & Bacon.

Tank, D. (2005, December). 10 ways to read an editor's mind: Increase your acceptance rate by carefully targeting a publication. *The Writer*, 49–50.

Tapply, W. G. (2005a, November). If you learned this in school, forget it. *The Writer*, 22.

Tapply, W. G. (2005b, November). Don't be a showoff. *The Writer*, 20–23.

Thoene, B., & Thoene, B. (1990). *Writer to writer: A practical handbook on the craft of writing from idea to contract*. Minneapolis, MN: Bethany House.

Tolkien, J. R. R. (2002). *The lord of the rings*. New York: HarperCollins. (Original work published 1954 and 1955)

University of Chicago Press. (2003). *The Chicago manual of style* (15th ed.). Chicago: Author.

Viguerie, R. A., & Franke, D. (2004). *America's right turn: How conservatives used new and alternative media to take power*. Chicago: Bonus Books.

Warren, L. (2004). *The savvy author's guide to book publicity*. New York: Carroll & Graf.

Weisberger, L. (2003). *The devil wears Prada*. New York: Broadway.

Wilson, L. (2003). *The copyright guide: A friendly handbook to protecting and profiting from copyrights*. New York: Allworth Press.

Zaharoff, H. G. (2005, November). Know your copyrights. *Writer's Digest, 47–50*.

Zinsser, W. (1985). *On writing well* (3rd ed.). New York: Harper & Row.

Index

About the Author

Kathleen A. Kendall-Tackett, PhD, is a health psychologist, an international board certified lactation consultant, and a research associate professor of psychology at the Family Research Lab/Crimes Against Children Research Center at the University of New Hampshire. Dr. Kendall-Tackett's specialty is women's health, and her research interests include the long-term health effects of child maltreatment and trauma; the link between trauma and chronic pain; causes, consequences, and treatment options for maternal depression; and the psychological aspects of breastfeeding. She is passionate about the importance of "translating" science, and her work centers on putting research into the hands of consumers and professionals working on the front lines of health care. Dr. Kendall-Tackett is the author of more than 150 articles or chapters and is the author or editor of 15 books on a wide range of topics. She is on the editorial boards of *Child Abuse & Neglect*, the *Journal of Child Sexual*

Abuse, and the *Journal of Human Lactation.* She is also the "Ask a Lactation Consultant" columnist on Pregnancy.org.

Dr. Kendall-Tackett received bachelor's and master's degrees in psychology from California State University, Chico, and a PhD from Brandeis University in social and developmental psychology. She has won several awards, including the Outstanding Research Study Award from the American Professional Society on the Abuse of Children, and was named Distinguished Alumna, College of Behavioral and Social Sciences, California State University, Chico.